Practice Tests for IGCSE in ESL
Listening and Speaking
Core and Extended Levels

Marian Barry

GEORGIAN PRESS

Georgian Press (Jersey) Limited
Pirouet House
Union Street
St Helier
Jersey JE4 8ZQ
Channel Islands

First published by Georgian Press (Jersey) Limited 2000

ISBN 1-873630-26-3 (without key)
ISBN 1-873630-27-1 (with key)

Produced by AMR Ltd

Printed in Egypt by International Printing House

Photograph (pages 28 & 58) by Judith Brown
Map (pages 43 & 69) by Art Construction

CONTENTS

Core curriculum

PAPER 1 Reading and Writing   (1½ hours)

(Grades available: C - G)

PART 1: READING SKILLS

3 reading comprehension exercises based on brochures/adverts and newspaper/magazine texts. On average, there are 5 questions per exercise. Question formats are short-answer for exercise 1 with either short-answer or true-false/multiple-choice formats for exercises 2 and 3.

Skills required

Skim, scan and read closely to extract information. Incline of difficulty.

Total marks: 15 (e.g. 5 + 5 + 5)

PART 2: INTEGRATED READING AND WRITING SKILLS

Exercise 1: Detailed comprehension text which may include information (charts etc) presented visually. Candidates answer about 5 questions. Answers to be sentence-length.

Exercise 2: Summary in 100 words.

Exercise 3: Fill in a form based on a given scenario.

Skills required

Detailed reading comprehension, including ability to understand statistical/visual information (ex.1).

Ability to write concisely in summary form using own words (ex. 2).

Ability to interpret a scenario and transfer information to a form as if candidate is the person in the scenario (ex. 3).

Total marks: 6 + 8 + 6 = 20

PART 3: WRITING SKILLS

2 composition questions.

Exercise 1 often has a visual stimulus (e.g. photos, picture, leaflet). Requires 100 words.

Exercise 2 may have a visual or verbal stimulus. Requires 150 words.

Contexts: formal/informal letters, articles for school newsletter/teenage magazine/newspaper.

Skills required

Write in connected prose, paragraph, punctuate, spell common words, use suitable tone/register, show audience awareness.

Total marks: 9 + 12 = 21

TOTAL MARKS FOR PAPER 1: 56

Weighting: 70%

Extended curriculum

PAPER 2 Reading and Writing   (2 hours)

(Grades available: A - E)

PART 1: READING SKILLS

3 reading comprehension exercises based on brochures/adverts and newspaper/magazine texts. On average, there are 6 questions per exercise. Question formats are short-answer for exercise 1 with either short-answer or true-false/multiple-choice formats for exercises 2 and 3.

Overlap with Core

Texts for exercises 1 and 3 are the same. Questions are generally similar, with one or two more challenging questions added.

Exercise 2 is different.

Skills required

Skim, scan and read closely to extract information. Incline of difficulty.

Total marks: 18 (e.g. 7 + 5 + 6)

PART 2: INTEGRATED READING AND WRITING SKILLS

Exercise 1: Detailed comprehension text which may include information (charts etc) presented visually. Candidates answer about 6 questions, the last of which requires a summary of about 60 words. Other answers to be sentence-length.

Exercise 2 : Summary in 100 words.

Exercise 3 : Either a further summary in 100 words or a note-taking exercise.

Overlap with Core

Text for exercise 1 is the same, but Core candidates are not asked to produce the 60-word summary to round off the task.

Exercise 2 is the same.

Exercise 3 is different (Core candidates fill in a form).

Skills required

Detailed reading comprehension, including ability to understand statistical/visual information and produce a brief summary (ex. 1).

Ability to write concisely in summary form using own words (ex. 2).

Ability to write a further summary or take a clear set of notes on a text (ex. 3).

Total marks: 10 + 8 + 8 = 26

PART 3: WRITING SKILLS

3 composition questions.

Exercise 1 often has a visual stimulus (e.g. photos, picture, leaflet). Requires 150 words.

Exercise 2 may have a visual or verbal stimulus. Requires 200 words.

Exercise 3 asks for arguments, opinions and views and the stimulus is usually verbal. Requires 150-200 words. Candidates often have to select from prompts.

Contexts: formal/informal letters, articles for school newsletter/teenage magazine/newspaper.

Overlap with Core

Exercises 1 and 2 have the same stimulus, but the word length is greater.

Skills required

Write in connected prose, paragraph, punctuate, spell words accurately, use varied vocabulary, present an argument, use suitable tone/register, show audience awareness.

Total marks: 12 + 16 + 12 = 40

TOTAL MARKS FOR PAPER 2: 84

Weighting: 70%

Core curriculum

PAPER 3 Listening   (approx. 30 minutes)

(Grades available: C - G)

PART 1: SIX BRIEF SCENARIOS

6 questions about information given in 6 very short, straightforward monologues/conversations.

Skills required

Identify one specific point of information for 5 questions. For one question, identify 2 specific points of information, e.g. a date and a time.

Total marks: 7

PART 2: TWO SHORT DIALOGUES/TALKS ETC

Candidates listen to 2 recordings (short formal talks, announcements, conversations etc) and fill in skeletal notes or close a gapped text with single words or short phrases.

Skills required

Pick out information from what may be incidental.

Total marks: 12

PART 3: TWO LONGER TALKS/CONVERSATIONS ETC

Candidates listen to 2 recordings (informal conversations or more formal talks) and answer true-false, box-ticking, or multiple-choice questions on each. Each answer is worth a half mark.

Skills required

Understand more complex meanings, views, opinions and attitudes of the speakers.

Total marks: 11

TOTAL MARKS FOR PAPER 3: 30

Weighting: 30%

Extended curriculum

PAPER 4 Listening   (approx. 45 minutes)

(Grades available: A - E)

PART 1: SIX BRIEF SCENARIOS

6 questions about information given in 6 very short, straightforward monologues/conversations.

Overlap with Core

3 scenarios and questions are the same, 3 are different and more complex.

Skills required

Identify one specific point of information for 4 questions. For 2 further questions, identify 2 specific points of information, e.g. name a place, give a reason.

Total marks: 8

PART 2: TWO SHORT DIALOGUES/TALKS ETC

Candidates listen to 2 recordings (short formal talks, announcements, conversations etc) and fill in skeletal notes.

Skills required

Pick out information from what may be incidental.

Overlap with Core

Recordings may be the same or they may be different. Candidates have to do more writing in their answers, i.e. complete notes more fully.

Total marks: 15

PART 3: TWO LONGER TALKS/CONVERSATIONS ETC

Candidates listen to 2 recordings (informal conversations or more formal talks) and answer about 6 short-answer questions on each.

Overlap with Core

One recording might be the same or it might be different. Core candidates have to tick boxes, and their questions are simpler.

Skills required

Understand more complex meanings, views, opinions and attitudes of the speakers.

Total marks: 13

TOTAL MARKS FOR PAPER 4: 36

Weighting: 30%

PAPER 5 (Core and Extended curriculum)
Oral Assessment   (15 minutes)

Candidates take part in a discussion with the examiner and possibly another candidate on a set topic. There are up to five topics. Typical topics, with prompts to guide the discussion, would be the rights and wrongs of zoos, holidays, winning the lottery, health and fitness, etc. Students respond to a range of questions posed by the examiner. The more able may also initiate discussion.

Extended candidates may, alternatively, be asked to 'Choose a topic', which has no guided prompts and requires more individual thought. There are five 'Choose a topic' questions to select from. These include controversial statements such as 'Money is the key to happiness' or 'Teachers should earn as much as film stars!'

Timing

The discussion lasts about 15 minutes. The first few minutes are a warm-up phase which is not marked.

Skills

Candidates are marked on a grid covering communication, pronunciation, vocabulary, structures and flexibility. The best candidates can deal with abstract or intellectual concepts and communicate freely, but do not need to be of native speaker equivalence.

Marks

A mark range of 0-30 is available. Grades available range from 1 (highest) to 5 (lowest).

PAPER 6 (Core and Extended curriculum)
School-based Oral Assessment

This is a coursework option in which oral work is set and marked by the teacher. Prior agreement from UCLES should be sought if the coursework option is being considered.

Further information about the IGCSE in ESL can be obtained from:

Cambridge International Examinations
1 Hills Road
CAMBRIDGE CB1 2EU
United Kingdom
Website: www.cie.org.uk

About the IGCSE in ESL

These Practice Tests are designed to give practice in the Listening and Oral papers of the Cambridge IGCSE in ESL examination. The exam is set at two levels, known as Core and Extended. The Core papers are aimed at lower-intermediate to intermediate students, while the Extended are for students at intermediate to upper-intermediate level. (See *IGCSE in ESL at a Glance* on pages 4/5 for a detailed overview of the exam.)

The separate papers for Core and Extended levels are intended to encompass a wide ability range and to allow all students a chance of being awarded a qualification and a grade which reflect their level of ability in English.

The exam is often taken as part of the IGCSE curriculum which offers a wide range of subjects. However, IGCSE in ESL may be taken as a single subject entry alongside another course of study or independently as a qualification in English. The exam can be taken at any age, although most candidates are about 16 years old. Students usually study for the exam over a period of two years, which allows time for them to develop both intellectually and emotionally.

The IGCSE in ESL qualification is widely recognised by universities where evidence of attainment in English is a requirement for entry.

(IGCSE = *International General Certificate of Secondary Education*)

About the Practice Tests

Like the exam, the material used in the Practice Tests aims to be international in perspective, culturally fair to students from all parts of the world, educational in impact and to reflect the needs and interests of teenagers. Exam tasks are realistic and similar to what students could be expected to meet at work, in training or in academic study.

The **Practice Tests** have the following benefits:

- They introduce students to the exam format.
- They allow students to experience a simulated exam under exam-type conditions, if desired, and to practise under timed conditions.
- They help to build confidence and to develop exam techniques.
- Gaps in students' learning and skills can be uncovered and remedied.
- Students can acquire insight into what the examiners are looking for.

About the Listening Tests

As in the exam, there is an incline of difficulty in the listening passages. The skills required range from listening for short, specific bits of information, to listening to longer and more complex monologues and discussions where students are required to interpret as well as understand.

Candidates hear each recording twice, with pauses between for them to write their answers and check their work. All the pauses and repeats are recorded on the cassettes, so no pausing or rewinding by the teacher is necessary.

Core and Extended

As in the exam, most of the recordings for both Core and Extended are the same. Differentiation of ability is achieved largely through the questions and question format. Core candidates do 'short answer' questions, complete very brief notes and do box-ticking exercises. Extended candidates do more 'short answer' questions and have more gaps in the notes to fill in. See page 5 of *IGCSE in ESL at a Glance* for more detail.

Topics

In addition to the short scenarios for Part 1, a broad range of topics has been chosen so that students, whatever their particular interests, will find something of real benefit to listen to and enjoy. Topics include life as an astronaut, the thrill of high-risk sports, playing truant from school, a mysterious archaeological find in Egypt, the potential of telemedicine and an interview with a child actor.

Voices

The voices represent a wide range of ages and backgrounds. To increase the international flavour there are occasional accents from outside the UK (e.g. Caribbean, Australian, American) as well as mild regional accents.

How will the Listening Tests help students do well in the exam?

The Tests provide familiarity with the exam by using similar types of listening passages and question formats. The recordings reflect the pace of speech and range of accents typically used. In addition, the material is lively and educational. It will help develop the underpinning skills, such as the understanding of issues and language functions, that the exam is looking for.

What is the best way to use the Listening Tests?

The Tests can be introduced at any time during the year. You may wish to use two Tests for general practice and integrate them into classroom work, and reserve two to be used as mock exams.

Make sure the students can hear the tape comfortably right from the start. There is an opportunity during the warm-up at the beginning of the exam for candidates to say if they cannot hear the tape properly. After that the invigilator cannot rewind or stop the tape unless there is a sudden emergency (e.g. a candidate faints).

If students find a particular passage very challenging, replay it as often as needed or come back to it some weeks later and try again.

How do Parts 1, 2 and 3 differ?

Part 1, Exercise 1
Core and Extended candidates need to identify specific items of information based on six very short scenarios. Typical scenarios are information about a train delay, or a telephone call to change a job interview time. Students need to practise getting used to rapid switches of voice and situation, and listening for particular things. Recorded announcements and messages, short situational dialogues and fragments of conversation are used to test these skills. Typical speaker roles are young friends, a teacher talking to a class, a ticket collector talking to a passenger, or a mother commenting on picnic plans.

Part 2, Exercises 1 and 2
Part 2 contains two note-taking exercises based on factual recordings. In both exercises students listen for specific information, and there is an incline of difficulty between the two. In Exercise 1, students may be required to write numbers, measurements, ages, nationalities, dates, times, common nouns or straightforward phrases. Examples of Exercise 1 passages in this book include a short radio broadcast about a 'fun run', and a talk from a policeman about staying safe from crime.

Exercise 2 is also factually based, but opinion and emotion begins to colour the content making it slightly more complex. The notes are a little more expansive, especially for the Extended level. The passages vary from a falconer talking about birds of prey to an expert advising students on taking a year out between school and university.

Part 3, Exercises 1 and 2
In Part 3 students listen for the general idea in a more complex talk and have to see links between ideas, opinions and attitudes. Core candidates answer true-false and multiple-choice questions, or are asked to tick only those statements which are true. Extended candidates answer 'short answer' questions and are asked occasionally to identify the speaker's attitude. Core and Extended candidates have one passage in common in Part 3 and one which is different. Examples of Part 3 passages in this book include the joy of gardening, a doctor talking about children's health, and the dangers of closed-circuit television.

Exploiting the listening material further

Students who can recognise a wide range of structures, vocabulary and language functions are likely to do well under exam conditions. In addition, remember that Extended level candidates may also need to identify speakers' attitudes.

An obvious way to use the Listening Tests is, of course, to ask students to listen to the individual passages and answer the questions. However, there are many instances of the features of natural spoken language in the Tests where it would be useful to rewind the cassette and replay language items so students have a chance to study them in context. Some examples are:

- Signals to show the speaker's thoughts and changes of direction, e.g. *Nothing could be further from the truth/As I see it/To my mind/but/in addition*

- Idiomatic phrases, e.g. *food for thought/broaden your horizons/on the spur of the moment/green fingers*

- Phrasal verbs, e.g. *come up with/get through to/build up*

- Advice language, e.g. *Make sure you/You should/One good way is to*

You could also ask *'How does the speaker sound?'* to focus students on particular intonation patterns, indicating amusement, doubt, pleasure, enthusiasm and so on. There are numerous examples throughout the passages.

Vocabulary

Topic vocabulary can be developed by stopping the cassette when interesting lexical items come up. You can ask students to define the meaning of an item and/or to find words and expressions of similar meaning. Collocations can also be explored. For example, the topic of weather in Test 3, Part 2, Exercise 1 contains the common collocations *torrential rain, high winds* and *freak thunderstorm*. Students could be asked which of the three adjectives can collocate with the other two nouns (answer: *freak*), and which are not interchangeable.

Grammar

Structural items can be analysed in a similar fashion. In Test 3, Part 3, Exercise 1 the speaker (an archaeologist) says *She must have been important*. You can ask *'Does the speaker know for sure, or is he stating an opinion based on evidence?'* In Test 3, Part 1, Question 3 the speaker says *I was told this town was great*. You can ask *'Do we know who told him?'*, *'Is it important who told him?'* to elicit more understanding of passive forms.

Advice on marking

Like the actual exam, the Listening Tests require students to show a correct interpretation and comprehension of the passage in relation to specific questions. Comprehension is tested by using different words or phrases in the questions to those spoken on the tape. Students have to understand, not just lift or match, to get the answer right. Whether students have understood correctly is the key criterion to awarding the mark.

Mark an answer correct when the right information has been extracted from the passage or the correct box ticked. Sometimes there is more than one possible answer to a question. This is shown in the answer key by the use of a slash/slashes. Information which may be included in the answer but which is not necessary for achieving the mark is put into brackets in the answer key.

Answers which are not in the answer key

Answers can sometimes be correctly paraphrased in a number of ways. Occasionally, therefore, students will produce answers which are different from the key, and you need to decide if the answer is close enough to be marked right. Under these circumstances, you need to check whether the answer makes enough grammatical and contextual sense in terms of the question and the listening passage. Further hints are given below.

Dealing with errors

Students may make specific grammar and spelling errors in writing their answers. In this case, you need to decide whether the errors affect the sense of the answer, as given in the key. Sometimes grammar or spelling errors occur because students are guessing answers: they have not understood the speaker or the question properly. At other times, they have genuinely understood the passage and question but are unable to write the answer completely accurately. You need to use your own judgement in awarding marks in these cases.

Marking spelling errors

The Listening Tests, as the exam itself, have tried to avoid targeting words for an answer which are problematic to spell. The word required cannot usually be copied from the rubric because a synonym will have been used. If students have misspelled a word, decide whether they are simply guessing the spelling and writing phonetically. For example, if the correct answer to a question is 'lightning', you may decide that the spelling 'lightening' should be allowed, not only because it is a homophone, but because, as a contrasting spelling, it is problematic – even native speakers could be confused. However, a student writing 'light' or 'lighting' should probably not be given the mark, as both the sound and sense are quite different.

In deciding whether to allow a mark when a spelling mistake is made, it is also worth taking into account the complexity and frequency of the word in question. Homophones of common, simple words, such as writing *flour* when *flower* is required, or *sun* for *son*, are not really acceptable. The spelling of irregular plural nouns can also present problems when marking. For example, if an irregular plural noun is essential for the meaning (e.g. *feet*) and a student writes *foot*, this would not be acceptable.

Marking grammar and vocabulary errors

Students may make errors of subject-verb agreement, use the wrong part of speech (*happy* for *happily*), use the past tense when the present is needed, or the wrong vocabulary item (*the dress was 'broken' for torn*), and so on. Don't automatically mark these answers wrong if the sense is correct within the context, and linguistic accuracy is not crucial. However, if the errors cause ambiguity in the meaning of the answer in relation to the passage and the particular question, and you doubt whether the student really understood, then the mark should not be given.

Length of answers

Students should write briefly and only what is required by the question. Sometimes candidates write down absolutely everything they've heard which might be vaguely related to the question, in the hope that something will hit the bull's eye! These kind of answers do not demonstrate the genuine understanding the test is looking for, and should not be marked right, even if the correct bit of information has been 'covered'.

About the Oral Assessment

There are two ways of enabling students to be assessed for spoken English. Both Core and Extended candidates can take either Paper 5 (exam) or Paper 6 (coursework).

What does Paper 5 involve?

Paper 5 is set by UCLES and the total duration is about 15 minutes. Schools receive an assessment package which contains 6 Oral Assessment cards (A–F) for candidates, with corresponding Examiner's notes. The cards set out topics or scenarios for discussion, and the Examiner chooses which card to use for each candidate. The card is handed to the student after a brief warm-up conversation. (The warm-up is not assessed.)

For Extended candidates, the Examiner may decide to use card F, which, unlike the others, requires the student to choose a topic from a short list and to talk about it for approximately 5 minutes. These exercises require more individual thought, as students talk without the aid of written prompts. The Examiner then asks a few questions at the end.

The Examiner is elected through the Centre, and must be a teacher approved by UCLES to carry out the assessment. IGCSE class teachers have the opportunity to become Examiners themselves if they undergo training. Successful completion of the training allows you, if you wish, to examine your own class and to send a range of samples to UCLES for moderation.

What about Paper 6?

Paper 6 is an alternative, coursework option. Teachers set and mark their own students' work and send samples to UCLES for moderation at times when it suits them. Teachers **must** obtain prior permission and accreditation to carry out the coursework option. The Oral Tests in this book are very suitable for use as coursework assessments for Paper 6, or you can make up assessments of your own.

Further information about becoming accredited can be obtained from *Cambridge International Examinations* at the address given on page 5.

What skills is the Oral Assessment looking for?

For both Papers 5 and 6, spoken English competence is assessed using a grid covering three elements: vocabulary, structures and fluency. Each element is marked out of ten to give a final total out of 30. The Examiner is looking to see whether the student can communicate effectively in a structured discussion around a topic. However, it is important to remember that the test is one of spoken English, **not** of subject knowledge.

Reasonable accuracy in the use of vocabulary and structures is needed if the best marks are to be awarded, but a few technical errors will not result in a lower mark if the overall impression given by the candidate is one of communicative competence.

About the Oral Tests

The four Oral Tests in this book are designed to mirror the exam format of Paper 5 in every respect, as well as being suitable as coursework assessments for Paper 6. They also provide rewarding and stimulating oral practice in their own right. Topics are relevant to students' interests, age group and backgrounds. They include such diverse areas as music, handicrafts, the future, homes and the power of goals.

What is the best way to use the Oral Test material?

You can choose those discussion topics which complement your own curriculum or, alternatively, use them to introduce students to new topics. The best way to treat each topic is as a framework for an interesting discussion which allows students to show you how well they can handle spoken English. It is not meant as a straitjacket. As in the exam, you can adapt the topic to fit in with students' interests, as long as you keep within the topic area.

The Tests can be used flexibly and introduced at any time during the course. You may prefer to integrate the first two Tests into your coursework and to use the other two as mock exams as the exam date approaches. If you are doing Paper 6 (coursework), you can use the exercises in this book for your coursework assessments when you wish. The Tests offer opportunities to develop functional and situational language which you can further exploit as part of your classroom work.

The Examiner's Notes are guidelines to help develop the discussion and to ensure that students are challenged sufficiently so that they have a chance of showing whether they can achieve the best marks.

You can work out your own questions, using the Examiner's Notes to guide you. There is no need to cover each and every prompt, or to use exactly the same questions or form of words with each student. Adapt your questions to the information and ideas each student comes up with, to ensure a fruitful discussion around the topic.

Structuring the discussion

Start the discussion with easy, straightforward questions and then ask more challenging questions as the conversation develops and students grow in confidence. It is important to ask some abstract questions so that students get used to being challenged. You will also be able to see whether they can handle more thought-provoking questions which enable them to achieve the higher marks.

Remember that students should be encouraged to put forward their own ideas on the topic, even if they are not covered in the prompts.

Helping students understand what the Oral Assessment involves

Give yourself the role of a weak candidate, then pick out a confident student to take the part of the Examiner and give him/her a list of prepared questions to ask you on the topic. Make lots of deliberate mistakes, and ask the class to spot what you are doing wrong. For example:

- Say nothing in response to a question.

- Answer just *Yes* or *No* and wait for prompting.

- Talk at length, mostly digressing onto an unrelated area.

- Include some glaring errors which confuse meaning, e.g. the wrong tenses or vocabulary.

- Ask for repetition of a question in an abrupt way, e.g. *'Please repeat'* rather than *'Could you say that again, please?'*

Building oral skills gradually

Build lots of opportunity for oral work of all kinds into the curriculum. The more comfortable and confident students are with the idea of speaking in a group, the better they will perform in an assessment. Pair work, group work, role plays, simulations, giving talks, question-and-answer sessions and so on are all valuable ways of building skills.

Give students practice in typical functional and situational language for taking part in a discussion, for example:

- how to disagree

- how to ask for repetition

- how to interrupt politely

- how to signal ideas and opinions

- how to signal changes of thought.

Remember, of course, that responding to questions is an important skill, so listening skills also need to be extended. You can use the listening exercises in this book to develop specific listening skills.

Running a mock Oral Assessment

1 Decide the running order of the interviews and whether students will be paired or seen individually.

2 Choose a quiet room if possible (e.g. not adjoining a playground), where you won't be interrupted or distracted.

3 Have a working tape recorder at the ready and some blank tapes – preferably unused ones.

4 Decide which exercises you will allocate to which students before they come into the room, reserving the 'F' exercise for the most confident and able. Skim read the Examiner's Notes and jot down any ideas of your own on the topic.

5 Decide how you want to frame questions, remembering that easier questions should be used at the start and harder questions as the topic develops.

6 Start the tape running. Put the students at ease as soon as they enter by smiling and using their name and showing them where to sit. Even though it is an exam-type situation, the atmosphere can still be pleasant. Candidates who are nervous and not helped to relax will not perform well.

7 Use the warm-up positively. This phase (which should last 2–3 minutes) is not marked and is included so that candidates have time to get used to the exam situation. Ask the students to talk a bit about themselves. If you already know them, ask them to tell you something about a sport or hobby you know they enjoy, or a project they have recently been doing in class which they liked.

8 The warm-up allows you to assess how nervous the student feels and to choose another exercise if you think it would be more appropriate. If a candidate is very confident, you could use a shorter warm-up.

9 Hand the students the exercise you have selected, and allow them 2–3 minutes to read it through and focus their thoughts. For exercises A–E, remember that they shouldn't write anything. For exercise F (Extended only), they can write a few notes. Before starting the main part of the assessment, ask the students if they have fully understood the exercise and if they have any questions they would like to ask.

10 Use the Examiner's Notes and your own judgement to guide the assessment. Begin with simpler questions and progress to the more difficult level of questioning. Avoid too many closed questions which can easily be answered by a simple Yes or No. Use open questions such as Tell me about/Can you describe/explain why/how/when/where. Try to follow up the candidates' replies, within the given framework of the topic.

11 Keep within the total timescale of 15 minutes, by discreetly checking your watch from time to time. (This is easier if your watch is on the desk in front of you.) It is important not to rush the student, but equally you don't want the test to ramble. There is nothing to be gained from overlong sessions, and you should manage to get enough to grade the students from about 8–10 minutes of examinable talking time.

12 Handle digressions by bringing students back to the topic. Don't allow them to wander off the point for too long. On the other hand, allow them time to think and formulate answers. Don't rush in and ask another question or dominate the discussion. Although you can prompt or paraphrase where necessary, you can mark only what students say. The more they say, therefore, the more evidence you have for your grades.

Deciding on grading

When grading, take an objective, balanced and fair view of the complete interview as a piece of communication. Don't award low marks if the student made a few errors but generally communicated well. Similarly, don't allow yourself to be swayed too much by someone who uses a few impressive phrases but whose overall control of language and ability to answer the questions was weak.

The following questions will also help you decide how well a student performed:

- If the interview were a real life situation, would the student have been reasonably clear and comprehensible?

- Did the student explain his/her ideas quite well?

- Was pronunciation clear enough so that you could follow what was said without undue strain?

- Were questions normally understood correctly, or did they often have to be repeated or rephrased?

- Did the student completely misunderstand a question and answer on the wrong track?

- Were the vocabulary and structures used suitable?

- Did the student contribute ideas of his/her own or ever take the conversation in a new direction?

- How well did he/she handle sophisticated concepts?

Paper 3, Listening (Core level) and Paper 4, Listening (Extended level)

Both papers have three parts and five exercises. You will hear every listening passage twice. Details of the papers are given in *IGCSE in ESL at a Glance* on page 5 of this book.

Doing well in the Listening papers depends on how well you can understand spoken English. Getting answers right depends on understanding properly, not just matching words together, as the questions often use different words and phrases to those used by the speakers on the tape. Simple things such as recognising and writing numbers and dates, as well as complex skills like understanding detailed opinions, are tested.

Tips to help you achieve high marks

- Practise listening to spoken English as often as possible by watching English-speaking films and TV, listening to songs in English, and so on.

- Make sure you know how to transcribe dates, numbers, measurements etc.

- Extend your vocabulary so that you recognise more unusual words and complex structures.

- Work at learning more idiomatic language, e.g. *green fingers*.

- Try to spell as accurately as you can (although wrong spellings may sometimes be allowed).

In the Listening exam itself

- Say at once if you can't hear the tape properly.

- **Read the question carefully** and circle or underline key words in the rubric, e.g. *how/why/ when/where/how much/how often*, to make sure you understand what the question is looking for.

- If you are given visual information, e.g. a simple location map, look at everything to get an idea of what it's about.

- You'll hear an introduction to the passage before it begins. Use this time to predict what the speakers might say.

- Don't worry if there are things you don't understand in the first listening. When you hear the passage the second time, it will be much easier to follow.

- Remember that you don't need to understand every word to answer the questions well.

- In the note-taking exercises, you often have to reorder words or find words of your own to complete the gaps. The notes should make sense when they are completed.

- The answers to **box-ticking questions** are always based on the passage. You can't answer from guesswork. The answers may depend on links in the passage, so try to follow the connection between ideas.

- In **multiple-choice questions**, read the stem and all the distractors through before making your choice. Remember, all the distractors are written to look correct.

- You may be asked to tick only the **true** statements. Make sure you follow this instruction accurately.

- **Keep your answers brief** and to the point. Don't write a phrase or a list when the question requires just one word, in the hope that you will cover the right answer!

- Listen for the way the speakers sound (happy? disappointed? doubtful?) to help you decide their attitude to the topic.

- Use the pauses to check your work. Ask yourself: *Does this answer really make sense in relation to the question and to what I have heard on the tape?* Correct any mistakes of grammar and spelling.

- Never leave an answer blank, even if you have to guess – your answer might be right.

Papers 5 and 6, Oral Assessment (Core and Extended)

Paper 5 consists of a 15-minute interview with the Examiner. Ask your teacher if the Examiner will be someone from your school or someone from outside. You may be asked to go into the test on your own, or you may be paired with a partner.

After a short warm-up conversation, which is not marked, you will be given a card marked A, B, C, D or E, containing a topic or situation and some suggested ideas. You will be allowed 2–3 minutes preparation time, and you will then take part in a discussion with the Examiner. You can't make written notes, but you are allowed to ask questions during the preparation period.

Alternatively, some Extended candidates will be given the F exercise, which requires you to choose a topic from a short list on the card. You will put forward your own ideas on the topic you choose, speaking for about 5 minutes. The Examiner will ask you a few questions when you have finished. For this exercise, you are allowed to make a few brief notes before you begin.

If you are doing Paper 5 (coursework) your teacher will arrange the test for you.

The exercises on pages 73–80 of this book will help you prepare for either Paper 5 or Paper 6.

How to do well in the Oral Assessment

Preparation

- Practise as much as possible, talking in pairs and groups, in class and after class. You can arrange mock interviews with friends where one person takes the part of the Examiner. You can use the exercises in this book for practice and, if you like, make up some of your own along the same lines.

- Try to increase your vocabulary and general knowledge about topics. Listening to talk shows or radio programmes in English is very helpful. Notice how people respond to each other or express their views on issues.

During the interview itself

- Relax and take deep breaths. The Examiner is not there to find out your language mistakes or to test your general knowledge. He or she is trying to have a conversation with you so that you can show how well you can speak English.

- The warm-up phase is to help you get used to the assessment situation. Remember, it will not be marked.

- Use the few minutes of preparation time to read the topic or situation calmly and to focus your thoughts around it.

- There are no right or wrong answers to the questions. The Examiner just wants to know what you think and to encourage you to talk.

- Listen to each question carefully and answer the actual question you are asked. For example, if you are asked about your last holiday, don't answer by talking about your holiday plans for this year!

- Avoid giving too many simple *Yes/No* answers. Try to explain your answers with more detail and reasons. For example:

  'Do you think smoking should be banned in public places?'

  'Yes, because it's bad for your health to breathe in people's cigarette smoke.' /

  'No, because it takes away the individual's freedom to behave as they want.'

- If you don't understand something the Examiner says, use questions like:
  Could you give me an example?
  Do you mean ...?
  Could you say that again, please?

- If you don't know the exact word for something, for example *lifejacket*, try to describe what you mean: *'the thing people wear on boats in case they fall into the water'*.

- If you are being assessed in pairs, remember to let your partner take turns in speaking.

- Try to listen and respond to your partner too. Comments like *'That's interesting'*, *'I'm afraid I don't agree with you there ...'* or *'I see what you mean, but in my view ...'* are supportive and suitable.

- Showing the direction of your thought is really helpful to the Examiner, because it helps him or her to follow what you are saying. Try to use language such as:

  I think/In my view/To my mind (expressing opinions)

  But/On the other hand/Nevertheless/Also/As well as (signalling direction)

  On balance/All in all/On the whole (summing up)

LISTENING TEST 1

PART 1

Questions 1–6

For questions 1–6 you will hear a series of short sentences. Answer each question on the line provided. Your answer should be as brief as possible. You will hear each question twice.

1 You hear a customer returning a pair of shoes. Why are they unsuitable?

.... [1]

2 Your fifteen-year-old cousin is complaining about a magazine he has been reading. What is wrong with it?

.... [1]

3 You have been asked to help plan a party. What does your friend need?

.... [1]

4 You are going to return your library books. What does your sister ask you to do?

.... [1]

5 The doctor is reassuring a patient about a skin rash. Why?

.... [1]

6 What warning does the swimming instructor give, and why?

(i) .... [1]

(ii) .... [1]

[Total: 7]

Exercise 1 Question 7

Listen to the talk from a police officer about ways to stay safe and reduce the risk of crime, then complete the notes below. You will hear the talk twice.

PERSONAL SAFETY

If you are visiting a place for the first time make sure you ....

and the exact address of where you are going. Always ....

.............................., including the arrangements for ....

When you use a bus by yourself, choose a seat .... If you are

walking late at night, keep to well-lit streets and avoid crossing ....

or waste ground or going down dark alleys. If you are lost, ask a policeman for directions or

.... for help. Keep your purse or wallet out of sight at all times.

To keep your home safe from burglary, never ....

your door key or leave it under a flowerpot or doormat. At night, it's a good idea to

.... Don't leave money or expensive jewellery where they

can easily be seen .... Get to

.... and if you are concerned about a stranger in the area,

tell the police. On the telephone, do not .... to an unknown

caller if you are at home alone.

Finally, ... can further protect your home, so discuss

this with your parents if you feel such measures would be helpful. Remember, however, that serious

crime is very rare indeed.

[Total: 6]

Exercise 2 Questions 8–13

Listen to the interview with an astronaut, then complete the notes below. You will hear the interview twice.

8   Training to be an astronaut involved

     (a)   ....   [1]

     (b)   experiencing weightlessness

     (c)   *learning to operate the spacecraft*

9   Experiments on various materials to be used in

     (a)   ....   [1]

     (b)   *developments in electronics*

10   John's aims in science education are to

     (a)   *make science more exciting*

     (b)   ....   [1]

11   As a result of school visits ....

     ....   [1]

12   People's attitude to science will improve if ....

     ....   [1]

13   Greater international cooperation and shared knowledge on future space projects would mean

     ....   [1]

[Total: 6]

Exercise 1 Question 14

Listen to this interview with a mother and her daughter Joanna about Joanna's truancy. Indicate whether each statement below is true or false by putting a tick (✔) in the appropriate box. You will hear the interview twice.

JOANNA

	TRUE	FALSE
(a) She had a specific reason for playing truant the first time.	☐	☐
(b) She had planned in advance to play truant.	☐	☐
(c) She usually took more than one day a week off school.	☐	☐
(d) She kept the fact that she was playing truant a secret from her friends.	☐	☐
(e) One teacher was aware of her mysterious absences.	☐	☐
(f) She felt annoyed when her parents found out the truth.	☐	☐

MRS WATSON

(g) She did not know that Joanna was having problems at school.	☐	☐
(h) She realised what was happening after a friend said she had seen Joanna leaving a park.	☐	☐
(i) She blames the school for not taking immediate action.	☐	☐
(j) They are helping Joanna study more effectively.	☐	☐
(k) Their relationship is now back to normal.	☐	☐
(l) Joanna is taken to school by car every morning.	☐	☐

[Total: 6]

Exercise 2 Questions 15–19

Listen to the interview with a psychologist talking about risk taking and complete the statements by putting a tick (✔) in the box next to the correct choice. You will hear the interview twice.

15 According to David, a safer and more controlled world has led to

A		the need to stay safe at all costs.
B		the need for a wider range of sports.
C		fewer people taking unnecessary risks.
D		the demand for risk-taking sports.

[1]

16 The benefit of risk sports, according to David, is that

A		they help people to avoid taking foolish risks.
B		they reduce aggressive tendencies.
C		they encourage an extrovert outlook.
D		they enable people to take risks in other ways.

[1]

17 Bungee jumpers particularly enjoy the sport because

A		they fall really fast at first, and then slowly.
B		they like the feeling of terror followed by an adrenalin high.
C		they like the high-risk reputation of bungee-jumping.
D		cranes, bridges or hot-air balloons are used.

[1]

18 People with extrovert personalities are more likely to take part in risk sports because

A		they enjoy the attention they get.
B		they enjoy overcoming anxiety.
C		they have a greater sense of adventure.
D		they enjoy the social side of risk sports.

[1]

19 Immigrants to America

A		wanted freedom at any price.
B		wanted opportunity and new directions.
C		came from boring home environments.
D		were prepared to take foolish risks.

[1]

[Total: 5]

CORE LEVEL

LISTENING TEST
2

PART 1

Questions 1–6

For questions 1–6 you will hear a series of short sentences. Answer each question on the line provided. Your answer should be as brief as possible. You will hear each question twice.

1 Your teacher is informing your class about a timetable change. Which room should you go to?

.... [1]

2 You ring your local sports centre and hear a recorded announcement. When will the centre reopen?

.... [1]

3 At the railway station, you overhear a ticket collector talking to a passenger. Why is her student card not valid?

.... [1]

4 Your aunt is expecting a friend to stay with her for a week. Why might the visit have to be postponed?

.... [1]

5 You need to take some medicine for your cough. What does the doctor advise?

.... [1]

6 You are returning a pair of headphones to the shop. Why will it not be possible for you to get a refund? Give **two** reasons.

(i) .... [1]

(ii) .... [1]

[Total: 7]

Exercise 1 Question 7

Listen to this science report about a new way to use solar power, then complete the notes below. You will hear the report twice.

Advances in technology mean that a cheap, ... source of electricity may soon be available worldwide.

Solar–powered satellites will change sunlight into electricity. The energy will be beamed to earth by microwaves, to be collected by a ....
....

Advantages of solar–powered satellites:
- **Take only 90 minutes to orbit earth.**
- ***Produce electricity very*** .... **.**
- **Less scattering and absorption of radiation.**

Advances in technology now mean that solar panels will be only 200 metres long and also .... , which will make launching them into space ....

Scientists believe that if the .... at the correct frequencies, people and the environment will both be safe.

[Total: 6]

Exercise 2 Questions 8–11

Listen to the interview with a person who works at a falconry centre, then complete the notes below. You will hear the interview twice.

8   Facts about birds of prey:

   (i) *370* different species in the world

   (ii) the birds catch food with their feet

   (iii) ....   [1]

9   The most challenging aspects of the job for Mike:

   (i) ....   [1]

   (ii) *building a trusting relationship with the birds*

10   Why there are fewer birds of prey now:

   (i) ....   [1]

   (ii) ....   [1]

   What the Centre does to compensate:

   (iii) ....   [1]

11   How the Centre teaches children about falconry:

   (i) ....   [1]

   (ii) *sends a newsletter to schools*

[Total: 6]

Exercise 1 Question 12

Listen to this interview with a gardener and indicate whether the statements are true or false by putting a tick (✔) in the appropriate box. You will hear the interview twice.

	TRUE	FALSE
(a) Mariella's house is similar to the other houses in the neighbourhood.	☐	☐
(b) Her garden is inspired by gardens in Jamaica.	☐	☐
(c) Her father grew sugar cane in Jamaica.	☐	☐
(d) The garden was not well-kept when she moved into the house.	☐	☐
(e) Mariella waited a few years before beginning to plant the garden.	☐	☐
(f) Her son liked to eat uncooked vegetables.	☐	☐
(g) Gardening reference books were an essential aid at first.	☐	☐
(h) She showed her grandson how to plant sunflowers.	☐	☐
(i) Mariella pointed out her gardening awards to the interviewer.	☐	☐
(j) Her prize-winning flowers were planted in a bucket.	☐	☐
(k) Her favourite Jamaican plant will not grow in England.	☐	☐
(l) The best part of Jamaica for her grandchildren will be a sense of freedom.	☐	☐

[Total: 6]

Exercise 2 Questions 13–17

Ian and Maya are discussing how their school could raise money for people affected by an earthquake. Listen to their conversation and complete the statements by putting a tick (✔) in the box next to the correct choice. You will hear the conversation twice.

13 People will want to support the event because

A they have experienced an earthquake themselves.

B some people lost relatives in the earthquake.

C the speaker from the charity was very effective.

D it will help raise money for the earthquake appeal.   [1]

14 According to Maya, the attraction of a quiz evening would be

A the prizes.

B the competitive aspect.

C the price of the tickets.

D making up the questions.   [1]

15 Ian would like a fundraising event which is

A different from previous events.

B as good as previous events.

C more affordable than previous events.

D better organised than previous events.   [1]

16 The success of the concert party they are proposing depends on

A   having excellent food and drink.

B   choosing talented performers.

C   advertising well in advance.

D   keeping the ticket prices reasonable.   [1]

17 The school grounds are not ideal for holding the party because

A   the kitchens are too far away.

B   there are no trees for shade or toilet facilities nearby.

C   there is no parking space for car drivers.

D   there are no benches to sit on or places to erect a tent.   [1]

[Total: 5]

CORE LEVEL

LISTENING TEST 3

PART 1

Questions 1–6

For questions 1–6 you will hear a series of short sentences. Answer each question on the line provided. Your answer should be as brief as possible. You will hear each question twice.

1 You telephone the cinema to find out the times of the programme. When does the evening performance begin?

.... [1]

2 Sam is asking the librarian to reserve a book for him. Which book does he want to borrow?

.... [1]

3 Ronnie has been ill. Why did he refuse to take the advice given to him?

.... [1]

4 Mrs Miller and her family are on their way to have a picnic in a country park. Why will they not be able to have the barbecue they planned?

.... [1]

5 Juliet is talking about her holiday. What was the best part of the trip?

.... [1]

6 Louise is ringing up to change a hospital appointment. Why can't she attend? What is she offered instead?

(i) .... [1]

(ii) .... [1]

[Total: 7]

Exercise 1 Question 7

Listen to the report about weather conditions across the world and complete the notes below.
You will hear the report twice.

The weather last week

Weather in general: Great fluctuations in temperatures.

Monday

Denver, Rockies: 21°C, 10 degrees above normal. .... conditions in

other places in U.S. and .... in Canada.   [1]

Tuesday

Cairns, Queensland: .... with 90 mm rain.   [1]

Wednesday

Johannesburg: .... °C, ... degrees above normal.   [1]

Thursday

Algeria: torrential rain, some floods.

Friday

Oman: freak .... lasting 6 hours.   [1]

Saturday

Central America: .... did not arrive but El Niño effect brought

.... and .... to many areas of the coastline.   [1]

Also caused by El Niño

Continuing drought in S.E.Asia.

Indonesia: *forest fires* much worse and increased levels of *air pollution*.

[Total: 5]

Exercise 2 Questions 8–11

Listen to this talk for school leavers who are thinking of taking a year out between school and university. Then complete the notes below. You will hear the talk twice.

8   <u>Advantages</u>

(a) Break from studying

(b) *Broaden your horizons*

(c) ....   [1]

9   <u>Effect on future employment</u>

(a) Future employers will ask ....   [1]

(b) Try to choose ....   [1]

10   <u>Overseas travel</u>

Research countries and find out

(a) ....   [1]

(b) ....   [1]

(c) ....   [1]

11   <u>Working abroad</u>

(a) Arrange employment before leaving country by *contacting agencies.*

(b) Popular jobs abroad include working ....

....   [1]

<u>University interviews</u>

Make sure you *are not abroad when these take place.*

[Total: 7]

Exercise 1 Questions 12–16

Listen to this interview with an archaeologist and complete the statements by putting a tick (✔) in the box next to the correct choice. You will hear the interview twice.

12 At this stage in the excavation, Tony and his team have

A		reached the entrance to the royal burial tomb.
B		reached the deepest part of the royal burial tomb.
C		slowed down for lack of suitable equipment.
D		become frustrated by the difficulties of the project.	[1]

13 Tony finds his job worthwhile, despite the discomforts, because

A		it is well paid.
B		it is highly respected.
C		he might make an exciting discovery.
D		he has made wonderful finds in the past.	[1]

14 The day before the interview was satisfying because

A		he uncovered evidence of an unknown woman.
B		the granite block turned out to be valuable.
C		the markings on the block were spectacular.
D		they realised the king had another daughter.	[1]

15 After leaving the site each day, Tony usually

A ☐ meets fellow archaeologists for lunch.

B ☐ writes up notes about what he has found.

C ☐ looks things up in the reference library.

D ☐ plans the following day with his colleagues. [1]

16 Tony's plans for the future include

A ☐ giving a talk on the radio about the Valley of the Kings.

B ☐ writing a book for the general public.

C ☐ talking to children about ancient Egypt.

D ☐ making a documentary about the Valley of the Kings. [1]

[Total: 5]

Exercise 2 Question 17

Listen to this interview with a doctor about young people and smoking. Indicate which statements are **true** by putting a tick (✔) in the appropriate box. Tick **only 6 boxes**. You will hear the interview twice.

(a) More teenage boys than girls smoke. ☐

(b) Half of young people will die from smoking. ☐

(c) Young people are usually unaware of the health risks when they begin to smoke. ☐

(d) The doctor believes there is no single cause for starting smoking. ☐

(e) The doctor used to smoke when she was a teenager. ☐

(f) Cigarette companies claim the aim of advertising is to encourage smokers to change to another brand. ☐

(g) Young people dislike seeing their favourite film stars smoking. ☐

(h) There is more smoking in films now than there used to be. ☐

(i) Parents usually try to stop smoking for the sake of their children's health. ☐

(j) A health problem was the reason the doctor's father gave up smoking. ☐

(k) The doctor wants to ban smoking completely. ☐

[Total: 6]

LISTENING TEST 4

PART 1

Questions 1–6

For questions 1–6 you will hear a series of short sentences. Answer each question on the line provided. Your answer should be as brief as possible. You will hear each question twice.

1 The headteacher has an announcement to make at assembly. Where should people wanting to register for sports training go?

.... [1]

2 Petra is looking for something. Where does her friend suggest it might be?

.... [1]

3 Suzanne is talking to her mother about the shopping she has done. Which item was more expensive than expected?

.... [1]

4 Martha is inviting a visitor to her country to a festival. What is the festival celebrating?

.... [1]

5 You hear this information on local radio. What website address do they recommend?

.... [1]

6 Mrs Taylor is ringing a friend to ask a favour. What does John need? Why?

(i) .... [1]

(ii) .... [1]

[Total: 7]

Exercise 1 Questions 7–11

Listen to this local radio announcement about a forthcoming 'fun run' and complete the notes below.
You will hear the announcement twice.

---

7   **Tenth Community Fun Run to be held on** ....

     Total number of entrants ....   [1]

     Participant details

8   **Laura Corville: Attends St Mary's High School. Will be** .... **on day of race.**

     Raising money for .... **at the hospital.**   [1]

9   **May Ayad: From Drayton. Hoping to beat last year's time of** ....

     Raising money for ....   [1]

10   **Thomas Meyer: From** .... **Raising money for Endangered**

     Wildlife Research Fund. Studying .... **at university.**   [1]

---

11 Mark on the map the following points :

     (a) Start (*S*)   **(b)** Finish (*F*)   [1]

     (c) First Aid service (*FA*)   [1]

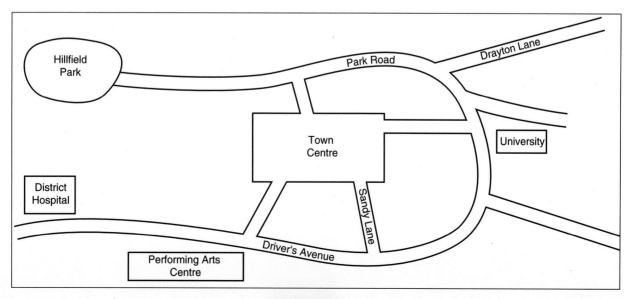

[Total: 6]

Exercise 2 Question 12

Listen to the radio interview about human survival and complete the notes below.
You will hear the interview twice.

Surviving Extremes

The human body can survive extremes of climate because

- physical characteristics have evolved over time

- every human being is able to .... [1]

E.g. we can .... when it is hot, we can *shiver* when it is cold, and we

can also cut down on heat loss from the body. [1]

- We have developed .... and .... which enable

  us to build suitable shelter, eat the right food and have protective clothing. [1]

Scientists believe that fossils found in Africa show that *human life began* there.

When people moved to cooler areas they took ....

with them. [1]

At high altitudes, people have adapted to *reduced levels of oxygen*.

A headache is the .... [1]

Special equipment still needed to survive underwater, because of pressure on lungs.

Japanese pearl divers have developed ....

to allow them to stay underwater for longer. [1]

[Total: 6]

Exercise 1 Question 13

Listen to this interview with a schoolboy who acts in a television series and indicate which statements are **true** by putting a tick (✔) in the appropriate box. Tick **only 6 boxes**. You will hear the interview twice.

(a) A story about Julian's music award appeared in a local newspaper. ☐

(b) The producer of The Star Game needed a fourth person. ☐

(c) Julian was sent to drama lessons before taking part in the series. ☐

(d) The cameramen invited all the actors to an end-of-series party. ☐

(e) Julian had no particular feelings about any of the cast. ☐

(f) As a child he was given the chance to train as a professional football player. ☐

(g) His weekend plans include playing football for his school team. ☐

(h) Music journalism appeals to him as an alternative career. ☐

(i) Julian listens to pop music when he is doing homework. ☐

(j) Piano lessons introduced him to the pleasures of music. ☐

(k) He is teaching his brother to play the guitar. ☐

(l) He believes that luck is the main ingredient of success. ☐

[Total: 6]

Exercise 2 Questions 14–18

Listen to this talk about an archaeological discovery and complete the statements by putting a tick (✔) in the box next to the correct choice. You will hear the talk twice.

14 The discovery was made by

A ☐ the police.

B ☐ children.

C ☐ tourists.

D ☐ scientists.   [1]

15 Clues to the age of the Iceman came from

A ☐ the age of the glacier.

B ☐ everyday objects found with the body.

C ☐ his skin.

D ☐ examining the skeleton through X-rays.   [1]

16 Some scientists think the Iceman's body was not attacked by animals because

A ☐ his body was first covered by a layer of snow.

B ☐ no animals are found at such high altitudes.

C ☐ the body was immediately enclosed in ice.

D ☐ the Iceman had fallen into a deep crevice.   [1]

17 The most interesting aspect of the Iceman's body is

A ☐ his unusual front teeth.

B ☐ the damage to his feet.

C ☐ his skin decorations.

D ☐ his odd internal organs. [1]

18 The Iceman's cloak is

A ☐ similar to cloaks worn until modern times by herdsmen.

B ☐ made of fur and leather.

C ☐ the least well preserved of all the items.

D ☐ in several pieces. [1]

[Total: 5]

EXTENDED LEVEL

LISTENING TEST 1

PART 1

Questions 1–6

For questions 1–6 you will hear a series of short sentences. Answer each question on the line provided. Your answer should be as brief as possible. You will hear each question twice.

1 You are waiting to catch a train to Westport. What is the cause of the delay?

.... [1]

2 A friend is talking to you about a school trip. What kind of trip was it?

.... [1]

3 You meet a neighbour. Why is she concerned and what is she going to do about it?

(i) .... [1]

(ii) .... [1]

4 You are going to return your library books. What does your sister ask you to do?

.... [1]

5 The doctor is reassuring a patient about a skin rash. Why?

.... [1]

6 What warning does the swimming instructor give, and why?

(i) .... [1]

(ii) .... [1]

[Total: 8]

Exercise 1 Question 7

Listen to the talk from a police officer about ways to stay safe and reduce the risk of crime, then complete the notes below. You will hear the talk twice.

PERSONAL SAFETY

If you are visiting a place for the first time make sure you ....

and the exact address of where you are going. Always ....

.................................., including the arrangements for ....

When you use a bus by yourself, choose a seat .... If you are

walking late at night, keep to well-lit streets and avoid crossing ....

or waste ground or going down dark alleys. If you are lost, ask a policeman for directions or

.... for help. Keep your purse or wallet out of sight at all times.

To keep your home safe from burglary, never ....

your door key or leave it under a flowerpot or doormat. At night, it's a good idea to

.... Don't leave money or expensive jewellery where they

can easily be seen .... Get to

.... and if you are concerned about a stranger in the area,

tell the police. On the telephone, do not .... to an unknown

caller if you are at home alone.

Finally, ... can further protect your home, so discuss

this with your parents if you feel such measures would be helpful. Remember, however, that serious

crime is very rare indeed.

[Total: 6]

Exercise 2 Questions 8–13

Listen to the interview with an astronaut, then complete the notes below. You will hear the interview twice.

8   Training to be an astronaut involved

     (a)   ....   [1]

     (b)   experiencing weightlessness

     (c)   ....   [1]

9   Experiments on various materials to be used in

     (a)   ....   [1]

     (b)   ....   [1]

10   John's aims in science education are to

     (a)   ....   [1]

     (b)   ....   [1]

11   As a result of school visits ....

     ....   [1]

12   People's attitude to science will improve if ....

     ....   [1]

13   Greater international cooperation and shared knowledge on future space projects would mean

     ....   [1]

[Total: 9]

Exercise 1 Questions 14–18

Listen to the interview about a new medical development called telemedicine, then answer the questions in the spaces provided. You will hear the interview twice.

14 What benefits does telemedicine have? Give **two** examples.

(i) .... [1]

(ii) .... [1]

15 Why can hospitals send patients home earlier after an operation?

.... [1]

16 How can telemedicine help medical students?

.... [1]

17 How can tele-psychiatry help psychiatrists diagnose patients' problems?

.... [1]

18 What did a research study into the effectiveness of tele-psychiatry find?

.... [1]

[Total: 6]

Exercise 2 Questions 19–24

Listen to the interview with a psychologist talking about risk taking, then answer the questions in the spaces provided. You will hear the interview twice.

19 Why does the psychologist think it is more difficult to experience risk in modern life?

.... [1]

20 Why are certain people attracted to risk sports?

.... [1]

21 What benefits can risk sports bring to those who do them? Give **two** examples.

(i) .... [1]

(ii) .... [1]

22 Why do some people avoid taking risks?

.... [1]

23 What is David's attitude both to people who take risks and to those who avoid them?

.... [1]

24 What kinds of people apply for immigration, according to the study?

.... [1]

[Total: 7]

EXTENDED LEVEL

LISTENING TEST 2

PART 1

Questions 1–6

For questions 1–6 you will hear a series of short sentences. Answer each question on the line provided. Your answer should be as brief as possible. You will hear each question twice.

1 You are taking part in an important sports event tomorrow afternoon. What kind of weather can you expect?

.... [1]

2 Helga and her brother are talking about buying a birthday present for their father. What sort of present do they decide he would prefer?

.... [1]

3 Zoe is ringing to change the time of a job interview. Why does she want to change her interview time? What alternative arrangement does she ask for?

(i) .... [1]

(ii) .... [1]

4 Your aunt is expecting a friend to stay with her for a week. Why might the visit have to be postponed?

.... [1]

5 You need to take some medicine for your cough. What does the doctor advise?

.... [1]

6 You are returning a pair of headphones to the shop. Why will it not be possible for you to get a refund? Give **two** reasons.

(i) .... [1]

(ii) .... [1]

[Total: 8]

Exercise 1 Question 7

Listen to this science report about a new way to use solar power, then complete the notes below.
You will hear the report twice.

Advances in technology mean that a cheap, ... **source of electricity may soon be available worldwide.**

Solar–powered satellites will change sunlight into electricity. The energy will be beamed to earth by microwaves, to be collected by a ....
.... **.**

Advantages of solar–powered satellites:
- **Take only 90 minutes to orbit earth.**
- .... **.**
- **Less scattering and absorption of radiation.**

Advances in technology now mean that solar panels will be only 200 metres long and also .... **, which will make launching them into space** .... **.**

Scientists believe that if the .... **at the correct frequencies, people and the environment will both be safe.**

[Total: 6]

Exercise 2 Questions 8–11

Listen to the interview with a person who works at a falconry centre, then complete the notes below. You will hear the interview twice.

8 Facts about birds of prey:

   (i) .... different species in the world   [1]

   (ii) the birds catch food with their feet

   (iii) ....   [1]

9 The most challenging aspects of the job for Mike:

   (i) ....   [1]

   (ii) ....   [1]

10 Why are there fewer birds of prey now:

   (i) ....   [1]

   (ii) ....   [1]

   What the Centre does to compensate:

   (iii) ....   [1]

11 How the Centre teaches children about falconry:

   (i) ....   [1]

   (ii) ....   [1]

[Total: 9]

Exercise 1 Questions 12–18

Listen to the interview with a gardener, then answer the questions in the spaces provided.
You will hear the interview twice.

12 What does the interviewer find surprising about Mariella's house?

.... [1]

13 What did Mariella's father do for a living?

.... [1]

14 Why did Mariella begin growing vegetables?

.... [1]

15 What was her attitude if seeds she planted failed to grow?

.... [1]

16 What made the interviewer aware that Mariella had won a number of awards for gardening?

.... [1]

17 Why did Mariella decide to enter the gardening competition? Give **two** reasons.

(i) .... [1]

(ii) .... [1]

18 Why is she taking her grandsons to Jamaica with her?

.... [1]

[Total: 8]

Exercise 2 Questions 19–23

Listen to the interview about how to get the best out of your memory, then answer the questions in the spaces provided. You will hear the interview twice.

19 Why is the expert opposed to the view that memory aids make your memory worse?

.... [1]

20 What is the interviewer's attitude to the idea that visual images help the memory?

.... [1]

21 What lifestyle factors affect the memory, according to the expert? Give **two** examples.

.... **and** .... [1]

22 Why is it helpful to use a mapping technique for taking notes?

.... [1]

23 What tends to affect everyone's ability to think clearly?

.... [1]

[Total: 5]

EXTENDED LEVEL

LISTENING TEST 3

PART 1

Questions 1–6

For questions 1–6 you will hear a series of short sentences. Answer each question on the line provided. Your answer should be as brief as possible. You will hear each question twice.

1 Mr Bagir is talking to a group of school leavers about his job as a car mechanic. What kind of experience is most useful when you are training?

.... [1]

2 A tourist officer is describing local attractions. What aspect of the area is most popular with tourists?

.... [1]

3 Ashraf is giving his views on the town he has recently moved to. Why does he like it? Give **two** reasons.

(i) .... [1]

(ii) .... [1]

4 Mrs Miller and her family are on their way to have a picnic in a country park. Why will they not be able to have the barbecue they planned?

.... [1]

5 Juliet is talking about her holiday. What was the best part of the trip?

.... [1]

6 Louise is ringing up to change a hospital appointment. Why can't she attend? What is she offered instead?

(i) .... [1]

(ii) .... [1]

[Total: 8]

Exercise 1 Question 7

Listen to the report about weather conditions across the world and complete the notes below.
You will hear the report twice.

The weather last week

Weather in general: Great fluctuations in temperatures.

Monday

Denver, Rockies: 21°C, 10 degrees above normal. .... conditions in

other places in U.S. and .... in Canada.   [1]

Tuesday

Cairns, Queensland: .... with 90 mm rain.   [1]

Wednesday

Johannesburg: .... °C, ... degrees above normal.   [1]

Thursday

Algeria: torrential rain, some floods.

Friday

Oman: freak .... lasting 6 hours.   [1]

Saturday

Central America: .... did not arrive but El Niño effect brought

.... and .... to many areas of the coastline.   [1]

Also caused by El Niño
Continuing drought in S.E.Asia.

Indonesia: .... much worse and increased levels of

....   [1]

[Total: 6]

Exercise 2 Questions 8–12

Listen to this talk for school leavers who are thinking of taking a year out between school and university. Then complete the notes below. You will hear the talk twice.

8   Advantages

(a) Break from studying

(b) .... [1]

(c) .... [1]

9   Effect on future employment

(a) Future employers will ask .... [1]

(b) Try to choose .... [1]

10 Overseas travel

Research countries and find out

(a) ....

(b) ....

(c) .... [2]

11 Working abroad

(a) Arrange employment before leaving country by .... [1]

(b) Popular jobs abroad include working ....

    .... [1]

12 University interviews

Make sure you .... [1]

[Total: 9]

Exercise 1 Questions 13–19

Listen to this interview with an archaeologist and answer the questions in the spaces provided.
You will hear the interview twice.

13 Where exactly is Tony working at the moment?

.... [1]

14 Why does he enjoy his job?

.... [1]

15 What was exciting about the discovery he made recently?

.... [1]

16 What does Tony usually do after lunch?

.... [1]

17 Why does he want to visit the Luxor temple?

.... [1]

18 What is his attitude to the media?

.... [1]

19 What does he want to do in the future?

.... [1]

[Total: 7]

Exercise 2 Questions 20–25

Listen to this talk about closed circuit television and answer the questions in the spaces provided.
You will hear the talk twice.

20 Why does the speaker feel that an ordinary person in the UK is likely to appear on a CCTV screen?

.... [1]

21 What example does the speaker give when he refers to small-scale CCTV?

.... [1]

22 When did the use of CCTV become more common?

.... [1]

23 The idea of filming people to prevent crime was put forward in the nineteenth century.
Why was the idea not taken up then?

.... [1]

24 Why does the speaker reject the idea that CCTV stops criminals committing crimes?

.... [1]

25 What is the main objection of ordinary people to CCTV, according to the speaker?

.... [1]

[Total: 6]

LISTENING TEST
4

Questions 1–6

For questions 1–6 you will hear a series of short sentences. Answer each question on the line provided. Your answer should be as brief as possible. You will hear each question twice.

1 Iveta is confirming arrangements for a flight to America. Which item does the travel agent remind her to bring?

.... [1]

2 Aysha and Peter would like to go swimming after school. How will they get to the swimming pool?

.... [1]

3 You are at a meeting about recycling in your neighbourhood.

(i) Where does the speaker want to put the recycling bins?

.... [1]

(ii) How often does he think the collection should be carried out?

.... [1]

4 Martha is inviting a visitor to her country to a festival. What is the festival celebrating?

.... [1]

5 You hear this information on local radio. What website address do they recommend?

.... [1]

6 Mrs Taylor is ringing a friend to ask a favour. What does John need? Why?

(i) .... [1]

(ii) .... [1]

[Total: 8]

Exercise 1 Questions 7–11

Listen to this local radio announcement about a forthcoming 'fun run' and complete the notes below. You will hear the announcement twice.

7	**Tenth Community Fun Run to be held on** ....
	Total number of entrants .... [1]
	Participant details
8	**Laura Corville: Attends St Mary's High School. Will be** .... **on day of race.**
	Raising money for .... **at the hospital.** [1]
9	**May Ayad: From Drayton. Hoping to beat last year's time of** ....
	Raising money for .... [1]
10	**Thomas Meyer: From** .... **Raising money for Endangered**
	Wildlife Research Fund. Studying .... **at university.** [1]

11 Mark on the map the following points :

(a) Start (*S*)   **(b)** Finish (*F*)   [1]

(c) First Aid service (*FA*)   [1]

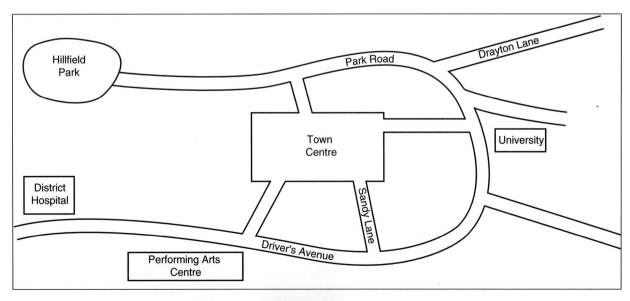

[Total: 6]

Exercise 2 Question 12

Listen to the radio interview about human survival and complete the notes below.
You will hear the interview twice.

Surviving Extremes

The human body can survive extremes of climate because

- physical characteristics have evolved over time

- every human being is able to .... [1]

E.g. we can .... when it is hot, we can .... when it is

cold, and we can also cut down on heat loss from the body. [2]

- We have developed .... and .... which enable

    us to build suitable shelter, eat the right food and have protective clothing. [1]

Scientists believe that fossils found in Africa show that ....

.... there. [1]

When people moved to cooler areas they took ....

with them. [1]

At high altitudes, people have adapted to .... [1]

A headache is the .... [1]

Special equipment still needed to survive, because of pressure on lungs.

Japanese pearl divers have developed ....

to allow them to stay underwater for longer. [1]

[Total: 9]

Exercise 1 Questions 13–17

Listen to this interview with a schoolboy who acts in a television series and answer the questions in the spaces provided. You will hear the interview twice.

13 Why did an article about Julian appear in the newspaper?

.... [1]

14 How did the director help Julian during rehearsals. Name **two** ways.

(i) .... [1]

(ii) .... [1]

15 What is Julian planning to do this weekend? Mention **one** thing.

.... [1]

16 How did Julian gain experience composing pop music?

.... [1]

17 Why is he helping his brother learn the guitar?

.... [1]

[Total: 6]

Exercise 2 Questions 18–24

Listen to this talk about children's health given by a doctor and answer the questions in the spaces provided. You will hear the talk twice.

18 Why Did Dr Harvey write her book?

.... [1]

19 What problems do the children who visit Dr Harvey tell her about? Give **one** example.

.... [1]

20 Why will one child react badly to a change of environment whilst another child will not be disturbed by it?

.... [1]

21 What advice does Dr Harvey give to parents and teachers?

.... [1]

22 What differences does she see between the children of today and the children of her own generation? Give **one** example.

.... [1]

23 Why is she likely to have more female than male patients?

.... [1]

24 How does Dr Harvey feel we should approach helping children?

.... [1]

[Total: 7]

Your Examiner will ask you a few questions about yourself to give you time to get used to the exam situation. This section will not be marked.

You will then be given a few minutes to read through and prepare for one of the following tasks. You are not allowed to make any written notes (except for Task F).

A Homecoming Party

One of your relatives is shortly going to return home after several years overseas. You would like to plan a party for him/her. Discuss with your partner or the Examiner what you will do to make sure the party is a complete success.

The following may give you some ideas:

– who to invite
– where to have the party
– music and decorations
– whether to tell your relative about the party or keep it as a surprise
– food and drink.

You are free to consider any other ideas of your own.

B A Memorial

Your town is planning to erect a memorial of some kind to an important person who has died in recent years. Local people have been asked to put forward their views about the kind of memorial they would like. Discuss with your partner or the Examiner the person you would erect a memorial to and the sort of memorial you would like to see.

You may like to consider such ideas as:

– the person who deserves to be remembered in this way and why
– the kind of memorial you would like to see
– the best ways of raising funds to build the memorial.

Of course, you are free to develop your own ideas.

C Rules at Home

Most families have rules of some kind. Discuss with your partner or the Examiner your views about rules at home.

You may wish to consider such things as:

– typical rules
– whether rules improve family life and, if so, why or why not
– suitable punishments – if any – for people who break the rules
– why some families have more behaviour problems than others
– whether TV and computer games have a bad effect on family behaviour.

You are free to consider any other ideas of your own.

D Staying Safe

Young children have to learn about safety and ways to avoid placing themselves in dangerous situations. Discuss with your partner or the Examiner ways children can avoid coming to harm.

You may use the ideas below, but you are also free to make up ideas of your own:

- problems associated with traffic
- dangers in the home
- dangers associated with playing outside the home
- dangers at school.

E Training for Jobs or Better Health?

Your town has a limited budget and has to decide whether to close either a training centre or a clinic. The training centre trains unemployed people in skills to help them find jobs; the clinic treats minor illnesses and injuries and carries out small operations. The town has asked local people which they think should close.

Discuss your own views with your partner or the Examiner.

F Choose a Topic (Extended level candidates only)

Choose one of the topics below and talk about it for about five minutes. The Examiner will ask you a few questions when you have finished. You may take a minute or two to write some brief notes before you begin.

1 Modern technology will give us all a better and brighter future.

2 The perfect home

3 We are all responsible for our own health.

4 The place I would most like to visit.

5 There is no point in giving money to charity because it only encourages people to be dependent on others.

Your Examiner will ask you a few questions about yourself to give you time to get used to the exam situation. This section will not be marked.

You will then be given a few minutes to read through and prepare for one of the following tasks. You are not allowed to make any written notes (except for Task F).

A Dream Holiday

Imagine that you have won a competition and are able to choose a dream holiday anywhere in the world (bringing friends or family if you wish). What kind of holiday would you choose and why? Discuss your ideas with your partner or the Examiner.

In your discussion you may wish to consider:

- whether you would choose a holiday overseas or in your own country
- the type of surroundings you would most enjoy
- the sort of activities you would most enjoy on holiday
- the souvenirs you would like to bring home.

You are free to consider any other ideas of your own.

B Recycling Rubbish

Your town council is concerned about rubbish in the streets and on open ground. There is a proposal to build a recycling centre for old bottles, tins and paper. Do you think this would be a good idea? Discuss your views with your partner or the Examiner.

In your discussion you could consider such things as:

- why rubbish can cause problems, especially in towns
- ways to collect people's rubbish for recycling
- where the recycling plant could be situated
- why some people may object to the idea.

Remember, you are free to discuss any other ideas of your own.

C The Future: Good or Bad?

Discuss with your partner or the Examiner whether you think life in the future will be better than it is now, or worse.

You may wish to consider such ideas as:

- the possibility of finding cures for diseases
- the state of the environment in the future
- how computer technology may affect people
- employment in the future.

You are free to consider any other ideas of your own.

D Smoking

Your town council is proposing to ban smoking in all public places. Discuss with your partner or the Examiner whether you think this would be a good or a bad idea.

In your discussion you may wish to consider ideas such as:

– why many people like smoking
– smoking and health
– advertising and smoking
– why young people start smoking.

You are free to consider any other ideas of your own.

E Water: A Precious Resource

In many parts of the world it is not easy to get clean water, whilst in other places water is taken for granted and often wasted. Is a clean, safe water supply across the world an impossible dream? Discuss your ideas with your partner or the Examiner.

In your discussion you could consider such things as:

– the many uses of water in everyday life
– why it is important not to waste water
– what can be done to make sure people in various parts of the world can get clean water
– the importance of educating people about water and health.

You may wish to develop other ideas of your own.

F Choose a Topic (Extended level candidates only)

Choose one of the topics below and talk about it for five minutes. The Examiner will ask you a few questions when you have finished. You may take a minute or two to write some brief notes before you begin.

1 The dream that everyone will have enough to eat *can* come true!

2 Why I want to be rich.

3 Space research is worthwhile!

4 People who fail at school have only themselves to blame.

5 There is no point in bringing children into the world today.

Your Examiner will ask you a few questions about yourself to give you time to get used to the exam situation. This section will not be marked.

You will then be given a few minutes to read through and prepare for one of the following tasks. You are not allowed to make any written notes (except for Task F).

A Clothes

Discuss with your partner or the Examiner your views about clothes.

You may wish to consider such things as:

- the sort of clothes you normally wear
- the sort of clothes you would like to wear
- shopping for clothes
- the cost of clothes
- different kinds of clothes for different occasions
- uniforms at school or work
- the idea of 'designer clothing'.

You are free to include any other ideas of your own.

B Food and Eating

Discuss with your partner or the Examiner your views about food and eating.

You may wish to consider such things as:

- the kind of food you normally eat
- your favourite food
- special meals for important occasions
- convenience food
- choosing a healthy diet
- cooking food.

Remember to include any other ideas of your own if you wish.

C Money and Society

Discuss with your partner or the Examiner your views about money.

In your discussion you may like to consider the following:

- the importance of money
- pocket money or allowances
- doing a part-time job to earn extra money
- the idea of a 'fair' or 'minimum wage' for work
- saving money
- becoming rich.

You are free to consider any other ideas of your own.

D Children's Behaviour

Some people say th at children today do not behave as well as they should. Discuss with your partner or the Examiner your view of children's behaviour.

You may wish to consider such things as:

- typical behaviour problems among children
- ways to encourage good behaviour
- punishments for misbehaviour
- how schools can encourage positive behaviour.

You are free to consider any other ideas of your own.

E Handicrafts

Handicrafts such as sewing, weaving, pottery and woodwork play a part in many societies. Discuss with your partner or the Examiner your views on the importance of handicrafts in society.

In your discussion you could consider such things as:

- whether you yourself enjoy making things with your hands
- the skills required for producing good handicrafts
- typical kinds of art and craftwork in your country
- whether people are less involved with handicrafts than they used to be.

You are free to include any other ideas of your own.

F Choose a Topic (Extended candidates only)

Choose one of the topics below and talk about it for five minutes. You will be asked a few questions when you have finished. You may take a minute or two to write some brief notes before you begin.

1 Everyone should learn a sport!

2 Celebrations

3 Friendship

4 The main problem with teenagers today is ...

5 Self-belief is the key to a successful life.

Your Examiner will ask you a few questions about yourself to give you time to get used to the exam situation. This section will not be marked.

You will then be given a few minutes to read through and prepare for one of the following tasks. You are not allowed to make any written notes (except for Task F).

A Enjoying Music

Some people say music is essential to life, whilst others have little interest in it. Discuss your views about music with your partner or the Examiner.

In your discussion you may wish to consider such things as:

- music you personally enjoy
- the reasons people have for listening to music
- different kinds of music for different occasions
- the value of learning to play a musical instrument or sing in a choir
- whether music becomes more or less important to us as we get older.

Remember, you are free to discuss any other ideas of your own.

B You and Your Home

'Home' may be a town flat or a house in the countryside. It may be a small cottage or a beautiful villa. Whatever type of home people live in, it tends to play an important part in their lives. Discuss with the Examiner or your partner your views about home.

You might consider such things as:

- the advantages and disadvantages of different types of homes, e.g. city flats, country cottages, etc.
- what you enjoy or dislike about your home
- what makes a house into a 'happy home'
- the kind of home you would like to have for yourself in the future.

You are free to consider any other ideas of your own.

C Friendship

Discuss with your partner or the Examiner your views about friendship.

In your discussion you could consider such things as:

- how we choose our friends
- the qualities that make a good friend
- making new friends
- whether making close friends gets easier as you get older
- tests of true friendship.

You are free to consider any other ideas of your own.

D The Power of Goals

Is having goals in life a good or a bad thing? What are your own personal ambitions and goals for your studies, your career, your sporting or social life? Do you eventually hope to become rich and well-known, or will you be content with a more 'ordinary' life? How are you going to go about achieving your goals?

Discuss with your partner or the Examiner your own goals and ambitions.

E Guilt

People who cannot feel guilt are said to be dangerous, but on the other hand some people who have done nothing wrong suffer from uncomfortable feelings of guilt. Discuss with your partner or the Examiner your views about guilt.

In your discussion you may like to consider the following:

- why it would be bad if people could not feel guilt
- where feelings of guilt come from
- situations that trigger guilt feelings
- whether women are more likely to feel responsible for everyone's happiness and therefore more likely to feel guilty about things than men.

You are free to include any other ideas of your own.

F Choose a Topic (Extended level candidates only)

Select a topic from the list below and put forward your own ideas on it for five minutes. The Examiner will ask you some questions about it when you have finished. You may take a minute or two to write some brief notes before you begin.

1 Pets

2 'Big business' and sport – a disastrous partnership!

3 Child film stars – exploited or just lucky?

4 Food just isn't safe to eat anymore.

5 Youth and enthusiasm are much more important in the modern world than age and experience.

TAPESCRIPTS

TEST 1, CORE

Part 1, Questions 1 to 6

For questions 1 to 6 you will hear a series of short sentences. Answer each question on the line provided. Your answer should be as brief as possible. You will hear each question twice.

Question 1 You hear a customer returning a pair of shoes. Why are they unsuitable?
I bought these shoes yesterday but I didn't have time to try them on. Now I think they're too tight for me. As you can see, they haven't been worn.

Question 2 Your fifteen-year-old cousin is complaining about a magazine he has been reading. What is wrong with it?
Mum got this magazine for me when she was out shopping, but I must say I'm disappointed with the articles. They're aimed at children, not teenagers. I won't be buying it again!

Question 3 You have been asked to help plan a party. What does your friend need?
I've been given permission to have my birthday party at home without any adults around. I'm organising it all myself. Could you let me have some of your CDs, as I don't seem to have enough music of my own.

Question 4 You are going to return your library books. What does your sister ask you to do?
Can you check whether the history book I ordered is ready for collection yet? I need it for my school project and it should be in the library by now.

Question 5 The doctor is reassuring a patient about a skin rash. Why?
You shouldn't worry about this red rash around your mouth. In my experience, it is never a sign of illness, although I know you probably feel a bit self-conscious about it.

Question 6 What warning does the swimming instructor give, and why?
Whatever you do, never at any time attempt to dive into the swimming pool, even at the deep end. The water looks deep but it's actually quite shallow, and you might hit your head on the bottom.

That is the last question in Part 1. In a moment you will hear Part 2. Now look at Part 2, Exercise 1.

Part 2, Exercise 1, Question 7

(Same as Extended level – see page 88.)

Part 2, Exercise 2, Questions 8 to 13

(Same as Extended level – see page 89.)

Part 3, Exercise 1, Question 14

Listen to this interview with a mother and her daughter Joanna about Joanna's truancy. Indicate whether each statement below is true or false by putting a tick in the appropriate box. You will hear the interview twice.

Interviewer: Joanna, perhaps you can start by explaining how you came to secretly miss school.

Joanna: Over a couple of months I got into a real habit of not going to school. The first time I played truant was because I hadn't done some coursework for my exams and I knew there would be trouble. I was waiting at a bus stop when a bus I didn't usually catch came along. I just got on it and ended up at the shops. I went for a coffee and wandered around for a few hours, then I went home at lunchtime. There's nobody at home during the day so I wasn't found out. After that I got into skipping school two or three days a week. My friend Sarah and I both missed school together one day. We went down to the park and had a real laugh with some other kids who were also playing truant.

Mum and Dad didn't find out for ages because the school only write home when you're away for three days in a row. But a teacher had noticed my absences and told me that if I didn't improve my attendance, my parents would be contacted. When that happened and a letter came, I got to it first and threw it away. Then the teacher wrote again and I was caught. Mum and Dad went mad, but in a funny way I felt relief that it was all over, because I knew I was going to get found out in the end and the problem was just getting worse.

I had to have an embarrassing meeting with my head of year, my teachers and my parents to sort things out. The school have been brilliant and are helping me work out how I can catch up with my coursework.

Interviewer: How did you feel about all this, Mrs Watson? It must have been very worrying, I'm sure.

Mrs Watson: Mmm. I thought Joanna was the last girl in the world who would play truant and was completely unaware that she was behind with her coursework. We'd never had a problem with her before. I did get a hint once that she'd missed school – a friend of mine said she had seen her coming out of the park during the day. But Joanna denied it, so I just accepted that my friend must have made a mistake.

When we first found out she was playing truant, we were angry that the school hadn't acted sooner. Now that we know she felt under pressure at school, we have been trying to give her more support with her homework and discussing what she's required to do for her coursework. But I feel that this has changed our relationship with Joanna and it will be a long time before we trust her completely again. We would really like to drive her to school ourselves but our schedules don't allow it. My husband has to leave the house at seven, and I go just after eight.

Now you will hear the interview again.

That is the end of Exercise 1. In a moment you will hear Exercise 2. Now look at the questions for Exercise 2.

Part 3, Exercise 2, Questions 15 to 19

Listen to the interview with a psychologist talking about risk taking and complete the statements by putting a tick in the box next to the correct choice. You will hear the interview twice.

(Same as Extended level – see page 91.)

TEST 2, CORE

Part 1, Questions 1 to 6

For questions 1 to 6 you will hear a series of short sentences. Answer each question on the line provided. Your answer should be as brief as possible. You will hear each question twice.

Question 1 Your teacher is informing your class about a timetable change. Which room should you go to?
This afternoon, your biology lesson will start at 2 o'clock in room 12 and finish at 3.45. I'll put up a notice in the science lab to remind everyone.

Question 2 You ring your local sports centre and hear a recorded announcement. When will the centre re-open?
The centre is closed for repairs from the 1st of July until Monday the 6th of August. We are very sorry for any inconvenience this may cause.

Question 3 At the railway station, you overhear a ticket collector talking to a passenger. Why is her student card not valid?
Although you've got an up-to-date student card, we can't accept it, I'm afraid, because it doesn't have a photograph with it.

Question 4 Your aunt is expecting a friend to stay with her for a week. Why might the visit have to be postponed?
I've got Dena's room ready for her but she's written to say her brother's very ill. She's not sure she'll be able to come until later in the summer.

Question 5 You need to take some medicine for your cough. What does the doctor advise?
This medicine is helpful in treating cough symptoms of your sort, but you must take it with food. It can cause a nasty stomach upset.

Question 6 You are returning a pair of headphones to the shop. Why will it not be possible for you to get a refund? Give two reasons.
Our policy is very strict with regard to refunds. These headphones have obviously been used several times, so I'm afraid we can't give you your money back. Also the box they came in has been damaged.

That is the last question in Part 1. In a moment you will hear Part 2. Now look at Part 2, Exercise 1.

Part 2, Exercise 1, Question 7

(Same as Extended level – see page 92.)

Part 2, Exercise 2, Questions 8 to 11

(Same as Extended level – see page 93.)

Part 3, Exercise 1, Question 12

Listen to this interview with a gardener and indicate whether the statements are true or false by putting a tick in the appropriate box. You will hear the interview twice.

(Same as Extended level – see page 94.)

Part 3, Exercise 2, Questions 13 to 17

Ian and Maya are discussing how their school could raise money for people affected by an earthquake. Listen to their conversation and complete the statements by putting a tick in the box next to the correct choice. You will hear the conversation twice.

Ian: It would be great if we could raise some money for the earthquake appeal. I think if we can hit on the right fundraising event, people will support it. Everybody's heard about the earthquake and and wants to do something to help.

Maya: Yes, I mean whole families have been wiped out – it's hard to take in. What really brought it home to me was when that woman from the charity came and described what it was like actually being there – you know, how people have lost their homes, their relatives. Oh, it's heartbreaking.

Ian: How about having a disco like we did last year? That was a big success. We raised money for the school trip, remember?

Maya: Mmm, but I think we should try to come up with a completely new idea. How about having a quiz evening.

Ian: What's that?

Maya: Well, you make up questions for a quiz and people are put into teams and the best team wins a prize. Everyone buys a ticket to come, of course. The prizes are usually just things like boxes of chocolates, but people love competing against each other. I think that's why quiz evenings are so popular.

Ian: I suppose it's a possibility but I just don't think it would raise enough money. We really need something a bit more unusual, that people will think is worth paying a lot to come to. We've done so much fundraising for good causes before that people are fed up with giving a lot of money to go to things which are – well – a bit boring, the same thing all the time, even if they <u>are</u> well organised.

Maya: I know – why don't we give a really big concert party? People could perform songs and dances, others could cook food, Samir could recite poetry, the school choir could sing. I think there's a lot we could do to entertain people, and they wouldn't mind paying a bit extra for the tickets for something like that.

Ian: Ah, now that sounds good. We've got a great choir and lots of other people with loads of talent. We need to give ourselves enough time to advertise it properly, though. That will be the key to whether it works or not. But where could we have a really big party? The school hall is too small. Ah, what about having it outdoors, behind the main building?

Maya: Ah, yes, I suppose it's not too far away from the kitchens, and we could put up benches and tables. Hmm, the only trouble is there are no trees to keep the sun off, and the toilets are quite a long walk away. But I suppose we could put up a tent on the grass, and there's plenty of space for parking.

Ian: Ah, let's see what the others think, then. And then we'll have to talk to Mr Dhanda and agree on a date ...

Now you will hear the conversation again.

That is the end of Part 3, and of the test.

TEST 3, CORE

Part 1, Questions 1 to 6

For questions 1 to 6 you will hear a series of short sentences. Answer each question on the line provided. Your answer should be as brief as possible. You will hear each question twice.

Question 1 You telephone the cinema to find out the times of the programme. When does the evening performance begin?
Our afternoon programme starts at 2 o'clock and ends at 5 o'clock. Evening shows begin at 6.45. No tickets will be sold after 7 p.m.

Question 2 Sam is asking the librarian to reserve a book for him. Which book does he want to borrow?
I'm afraid there's quite a waiting list for that business studies book. I can't let you have it until Tuesday at the earliest, as there are two other students waiting to borrow it.

Question 3 Ronnie has been ill. Why did he refuse to take the advice given to him?
I went to see the doctor about my sore ear. He said I ought to give up swimming for a month which I'm certainly not going to do. I'm training for a big competition.

Question 4 Mrs Miller and her family are on their way to have a picnic in a country park. Why will they not be able to have the barbecue they planned?

Mr Miller: Oh no! Did you see that sign over there? It says 'No barbecues due to risk of forest fires', so no hot food for us!

Mrs Miller: Good thing I packed some cheese. We'll just have to eat that with the bread.

Question 5 Juliet is talking about her holiday. What was the best part of the trip?
We had wonderful weather so we did plenty of swimming and sunbathing. But the most memorable bit was the camel ride through the desert – it was brilliant!

Question 6 Louise is ringing up to change a hospital appointment. Why can't she attend? What is she offered instead?

Louise: I've got an appointment with Doctor Brady at 10 o'clock on Thursday morning, but I'm taking an exam then. Is it possible to have a different time?

Receptionist: Oh, I see. Erm, thank you for letting us know. I'm afraid Doctor Brady's completely booked up this week. Could you come next Monday at 11.30 instead.

That is the last question in Part 1. In a moment you will hear Part 2. Now look at Part 2, Exercise 1.

Part 2, Exercise 1, Question 7

(Same as Extended level – see page 96.)

Part 2, Exercise 2, Questions 8 to 11

(Same as Extended level – see page 97.)

Part 3, Exercise 1, Questions 12 to 16

Listen to this interview with an archaeologist and complete the statements by putting a tick in the box next to the correct choice. You will hear the interview twice.

(Same as Extended level – see page 97.)

Part 3, Exercise 2, Question 17

Listen to this interview with a doctor about young people and smoking. Indicate which statements are true by putting a tick in the appropriate box. Tick only 6 boxes. You will hear the interview twice.

Interviewer: How many youngsters actually smoke in this country, Dr Lee?

Doctor: About 2% of 12-year-old boys and 4% of 12-year-old girls. But by the age of fourteen, this increases to 13% of boys and 24% of girls. The number of young people smoking is rising, and the sad truth is that half of them will die from tobacco-related diseases if they carry on.

Interviewer: Do we know why young people start smoking? Surely they know it's bad for them?

Doctor: They certainly do. 84% of children who smoke agree that smoking is harmful to health. There is a range of factors involved in the taking up of smoking. A lot depends on your situation. Many teenagers think it makes them look mature and attractive; it makes them feel independent; or they think it helps keep them slim. Most children who smoke regularly say most of their friends smoke, and they say it's hard not to smoke if most of your friends do. I was a smoker myself in my teens, and I think the main reason I started was pressure from friends.

Interviewer: What about advertising? Does it really encourage people to smoke?

Doctor: Yes, it does. Why else would tobacco companies pay for adverts? If companies are to stay in business, they need to make sure there are plenty of new, young smokers coming along, developing a lifelong habit. Of course, they argue that their adverts are simply intended to make existing smokers change their brand of cigarettes, and that they don't want to encourage young people to actually start smoking. But somehow the argument is not supported by the facts.

Interviewer: Is there any evidence that smoking in films encourages the habit?

Doctor: Yes, indeed. Research shows that young people often copy their favourite stars' habits, and that they are influenced by glamorous images of smoking.

Interviewer: But are there many images of smoking in films nowadays?

Doctor: Well, smoking in films is on the increase again. In 1995, box office hits showed four times as much smoking as in 1990.

Interviewer: There's been a lot of debate about passive smoking. What's the latest thinking? Can other people's smoking affect you.

Doctor: Yes. We know that passive smoking can cause a whole range of health problems. Children whose parents smoke inhale the equivalent of up to 150 cigarettes per year – but even that isn't enough incentive for parents to give up the habit. Of course, it's not easy. My father was a smoker for most of his life, and only managed to kick the habit when he developed asthma.

Interviewer: Finally doctor, what changes would you like to see?

Doctor: Cigarette advertising banned and a ban on smoking in all public places.

Now you will hear the interview again.

That is the end of Part 3, and of the test.

TEST 4, CORE

Part 1, Questions 1 to 6

For questions 1 to 6 you will hear a series of short sentences. Answer each question on the line provided. Your answer should be as brief as possible. You will hear each question twice.

Question 1 The headteacher has an announcement to make at assembly. Where should people wanting to register for sports training go?
We're very lucky to have a professional sports coach visiting the school for a few weeks. If you are interested in signing up to improve your skills, please go to the gym this lunchtime.

Question 2 Petra is looking for something. Where does her friend suggest it might be?

Petra: Has anyone seen my pencil case? I'm sure I left it on my desk with my books.

Friend: Have you looked through the lost property box? I found my school jumper there yesterday.

Question 3 Suzanne is talking to her mother about the shopping she has done. Which item was more expensive than expected?
I got everything on the list except the strawberries because they looked really over-ripe, so I got a melon instead. I had just enough left to get the washing powder too, but the price has really gone up since last week.

Question 4 Martha is inviting a visitor to her country to a festival. What is the festival celebrating?
Have you heard about the festival in the marketplace on Saturday? Everyone is going to dress up in historical costumes to celebrate one hundred years of independence. It sounds great. Would you like to come with us?

Question 5 You hear this information on local radio. What website address do they recommend?
And finally, for explanations in simple English about how hundreds of things work, from car engines to the internet, don't miss this extremely useful website: www.howstuffworks.com. That's our tip for the week. More next Tuesday ...

Question 6 Mrs Taylor is ringing a friend to ask a favour. What does John need? Why?
Sorry to trouble you, Eileen, but could you possibly call for John on your way to work and give him a lift to school? He hurt his leg playing basketball at the weekend. The nurse who bandaged it said he was very lucky not to have broken it.

That is the last question in Part 1. In a moment you will hear Part 2. Now look at Part 2, Exercise 1.

Part 2, Exercise 1, Questions 7 to 11

(Same as Extended level – see page 100.)

Part 2, Exercise 2, Question 12

(Same as Extended level – see page 100.)

Part 3, Exercise 1, Question 13

Listen to this interview with a schoolboy who acts in a television series and indicate which statements are true by putting a tick in the appropriate box. Tick only 6 boxes. You will hear the interview twice.

(Same as Extended level – see page 101.)

Part 3, Exercise 2, Questions 14 to 18

Listen to this talk about an archaeological discovery and complete the statements by putting a tick in the box next to the correct choice. You will hear the talk twice.

The body of a hunter which is thought to be about 5000 years old was found by two German climbers on the last day of their holidays in the Alps. At an altitude of about 3,200 metres they spotted what they first thought was a doll's head sticking out of the frozen snow. When they looked more closely they realised it was a human head and body with yellowish-brown skin. The tourists took a photograph and reported the find to the police. Eventually the authorities removed the body to Innsbruck. Although it was suspected to be old, nobody at first realised just how ancient it was.

Accurate estimates of the age of the body were based on the primitive tools, equipment and clothing which accompanied the hunter, or

Iceman as he came to be called. These estimates suggested that the body was in fact extremely old, and therefore rather valuable. The Iceman is the first prehistoric human ever to be discovered with his clothing and equipment intact, presumably going about his normal business. The body is in a remarkably fine condition. The pathologist who removed it from the glacier said that he was amazed at the degree of preservation. One theory is that, after the man died, his body was quickly hidden by a covering of snow, which is why it was not preyed upon by animals wandering in the area. In time, the body was sealed in ice, which led to its preservation.

Scientific reports suggest that the hunter was a dark-skinned male, between 25 and 40 years old, weighing about 48 kilos. His front teeth are very worn, which may suggest that he ate coarse-grained bread or that he used his teeth as a tool. His internal organs are in fine condition and there are just a few traces of arthritis in his feet. The most fascinating feature of his body is his skin decorations, which are rarely seen by archaeologists. He has what could be an earring fitted to his ear lobe, and he has various tattoos.

Many objects were found with the body, including an axe, a dagger and a bow and arrows. Among the clothes found were a rain cloak of woven grass, remarkably similar to cloaks worn by herdsmen of the region until very recently, and shoes which were packed with straw. He also had a fur cap with a leather strap. Whether he wore leather trousers or a fur and leather skirt is still disputed by experts trying to piece together the many fragments of material found by the body.

The Iceman is very expensive to preserve, and there are continuing arguments about the best ways to handle the find. One leading scientist working on the project said 'The Iceman brings us no money but costs us a fortune. Sometimes I think we should get a shovel and just bury him again!'

Now you will hear the talk again.

That is the end of Part 3, and of the test.

TEST 1, EXTENDED

Part 1, Questions 1 to 6

For questions 1 to 6 you will hear a series of short sentences. Answer each question on the line provided. Your answer should be as brief as possible. You will hear each question twice.

Question 1 You are waiting to catch a train to Westport. What is the cause of the delay?
We apologise to passengers waiting for the Westport express. The train will leave in 35 minutes. The reason for the delay is connected with problems in the engine.

Question 2 A friend is talking to you about a school trip. What kind of trip was it?
Well, we've just got back from our camping trip in Everdene Forest. We went for a week and had a great time. We slept in tents for four people, and did all our cooking over a fire. It rained a few times, but we didn't really mind.

Question 3 You meet a neighbour. Why is she concerned and what is she going to do about it?
It's happened again! Some children have been throwing stones at my dog. He hasn't been hurt, luckily, but I'm so angry about it. I'm going to report the matter to the police and let them have a word with the kids.

Question 4 You are going to return your library books. What does your sister ask you to do?
Can you check whether the history book I ordered is ready for collection yet? I need it for my school project and it should be in the library by now.

Question 5 The doctor is reassuring a patient about a skin rash. Why?
You shouldn't worry about this red rash around your mouth. In my experience, it's never a sign of illness, although I know you probably feel a bit self-conscious about it.

Question 6 What warning does the swimming instructor give, and why?
Whatever you do, never at any time attempt to dive into the swimming pool, even at the deep end. The water looks deep but it's actually quite shallow and you might hit your head on the bottom.

That is the last question in Part 1. In a moment you will hear Part 2. Now look at Part 2, Exercise 1.

Part 2, Exercise 1, Question 7

Listen to the talk from a police officer about ways to stay safe and reduce the risk of crime, then complete the notes below. You will hear the talk twice.

Good evening, everyone. I'm here today to explain some simple rules which will help increase your personal safety.

Firstly, if you are going out at night to a place you haven't been to before, make sure you know the route and, of course, the exact address of where you're going. It's surprising how many young people set off with just a rough idea of how to get to their destination.

Before you leave the house, you should of course tell your parents where you're going and the kind of arrangements you've made for the return journey. This may be a bus, taxi, lift, or whatever. Just be sure you know how you will get home. Leave a contact address and phone number too.

If you're going to take a bus by yourself, choose a seat close to the driver, especially if the bus is rather empty. If you're walking late at night, keep to well-lit streets and avoid crossing parks or waste ground or going down dark alleys. It's just common sense, really.

If you do happen to get lost, ask a policeman for directions or go into a shop for help. Keep your purse or wallet out of sight at all times, and limit the amount of cash you carry around with you. Remember – it's better not to create temptation for a thief, and most crimes are committed on the spur of the moment.

Now, at home you can increase your security and keep your house safe from burglary by taking care of your front door key. Never, for example, write your address on your door key or hide it under a flowerpot or doormat – this is the first place a thief might look! At night, it's usually a good idea to draw your curtains.

Don't leave money or expensive jewellery lying around at home, and certainly not where they can easily be seen through the window. Get to know your neighbours and if you see anyone suspicious – a stranger in the area, for instance – report it to the police.

Now, if you answer the telephone, do not give your name to an unknown caller or say if you're in the house on your own.

Finally, things like gates and window locks can further protect your home and deter a burglar, so do discuss this with your parents if you think such measures would be helpful. But do remember that serious crime against people is very rare indeed, so don't worry unduly.

Now you will hear the talk again.

That is the end of Exercise 1. In a moment you will hear Exercise 2. Now look at the questions for Exercise 2.

Part 2, Exercise 2, Questions 8 to 13

Listen to the interview with an astronaut, then complete the notes below. You will hear the interview twice.

Interviewer: Our guest today is someone who has seen the world from an unusual perspective. I'd like to welcome astronaut John Bellinger. John, I believe you were listening to the radio in the car when you first heard about a job vacancy in the space project?

John: That's right. I applied and to my amazement I was selected from thousands of applicants and sent to Russia to train.

Interviewer: What did your training consist of?

John: I had to go through a very rigorous physical fitness programme. You need to be very fit and healthy to undergo the rigours of space exploration. Er, in space you experience weightlessness whilst orbiting earth and I had to undergo tests to simulate weightlessness – this was very strange at first. Er, another important part of the training was learning about the technical aspects of space travel. There were only three of us who were going to operate the spacecraft, so I was trained to use all the systems. This meant that if there was an emergency I could do it on my own.

Interviewer: How did you manage a daily routine once on the spacecraft?

John: Well, living aboard the spacecraft was not as daunting as it sounds. Eating wasn't too difficult. We sucked coffee and tea out of tubes, and ate a lot of canned food.

Interviewer: What was the purpose of the trip?

John: Well, we carried out experiments on various materials to be used in new drugs and for developments in electronics. The results of the experiments were brought back to earth to be analysed and these are now availabable.

Interviewer: What kind of things are you doing now that you're back on earth?

John: At the moment I'm very interested in science education – trying to help teachers make science more exciting. I also aim to encourage schools to put space research on the curriculum – I think that would be a very good way to introduce a lot of basic scientific concepts. The feedback I've been getting from the schools where I've talked about the future of science is that more pupils are considering a career in science, which they wouldn't have dreamed of before.

Interviewer: Do you think scientists have suffered from a negative image?

John: To some extent, yes – perhaps because science has attracted shy, retiring people who are not great communicators. We really need scientists who can communicate well with others if the public's attitude to science is to improve. Unfortunately, scientists are not always the best ambassadors for their subject.

Interviewer: How do you see the future of space research?

John: Ambitious space projects need international cooperation. I'd like to see a world space station, involving as many countries as possible, including Russia and America, of course. They have a huge fund of knowledge about how to sustain people in space and the best kinds of space technology. If knowledge could be shared, in the end the whole world would benefit.

Interviewer: Well, thank you very much, John. I wonder what our listeners think?

Now you will hear the interview again.

That is the end of Part 2. In a moment you will hear Part 3. Now look at the questions for Part 3, Exercise 1.

Part 3, Exercise 1, Questions 14 to 18

Listen to the interview about a new medical development called telemedicine, then answer the questions in the spaces provided. You will hear the interview twice.

Interviewer: Technology progresses more rapidly each day. One interesting development in the field of medicine is the use of telemedicine. Doctor Lucas, what can you tell us about telemedicine, and how will it affect health management in the future?

Doctor: Telemedicine is the practice of medicine at a distance. It involves video technology and high-speed digital communications. Telemedicine has obvious benefits in remote parts of the world where it is very difficult to get to a doctor or a hospital. A small rural clinic which has a telemedicine video link, a satellite phone and a computer can give patients access, through the technology, to highly-qualified hospital specialists who can diagnose certain problems immediately. For example, a nurse or a doctor can focus a hand-held video camcorder on a patient's injury and show the specialist the patient's problem. The specialist can then immediately recommend a course of treatment.

Telemedicine also allows patients access to the best doctors and specialists in the world without ever leaving their home country. For example, a doctor in South America who specialises in rare heart diseases can now, using telemedicine, diagnose a patient in the Far East or India. This gives patients the chance of consultations with specialists from all over the world without having to travel to see them.

Interviewer: It sounds rather wonderful in a futuristic way, but won't it all be rather expensive?

Doctor: It depends how you look at it. In some ways, telemedicine will cut costs. For instance, patients recovering from operations can leave hospital much sooner because they can be monitored at a distance by means of telemedicine. This will certainly reduce the cost of looking after them in hospital, which is very expensive.

Interviewer: Is telemedicine going to be used in medical training in any way?

Doctor: It already is. And certainly telemedicine has a very useful role to play in bringing the expertise of the world's foremost specialists to medical students everywhere. Students in many countries can now watch a famous surgeon actually performing surgical techniques by video link.

Interviewer: It looks as though telemedicine is here to stay then?

Doctor: Certainly. Telemedicine has many far-reaching implications – in all areas of health. Mentally ill patients needing psychiatric help or those needing professional counselling can be helped through tele-psychiatry. This technique enables psychiatrists to actually see the patient and thus gain important clues for diagnosis from facial expression, dress and mannerisms. Tele-psychiatry has been successful in remote areas where the nearest psychiatrist is hundreds of miles away. More than half of patients in one research study said it had helped them understand their problems far better than they would have done without access to specialised help. And of course they can always switch off the telemedicine link if they don't like what they hear!

Interviewer: It sounds fascinating, and I for one could talk about it all day, but once again we are running out of time and so ...

Now you will hear the interview again.

That is the end of Exercise 1. In a moment you will hear Exercise 2. Now look at the questions for Exercise 2.

Part 3, Exercise 2, Questions 19 to 24

Listen to the interview with a psychologist talking about risk taking, then answer the questions in the spaces provided. You will hear the interview twice.

Interviewer: Why are some people prepared to risk all while others are happy to sit at home watching TV? Here this morning to talk about the strange phenomenon of risk taking for the sheer excitement of it is David Viscardi, a psychologist who specialises in risk. He has recently written a book, 'The Risk Phenomenon'. David, why is it that some people seem to crave adventure and excitement?

David: Many of us live in a world which has eliminated risk and tries to guarantee safety. This emphasis on safety at all costs starts to seem boring to – shall we call them – the sensation seekers of our time. Many people still need excitement and find normal everyday life much too dull. They turn to risk sports as an escape.

Interviewer: Are you saying risk sports like bungee-jumping or white-water rafting have a beneficial side?

David: Oh yes! These sports empower people to overcome fears that inhibit them in their real lives. When you do a risk sport you force yourself to do something very scary, but at the same time you learn that being frightened does not mean you are out of control. Er, lots of people say they would like to start a business, for example, but they don't have the courage. Risk sports help them develop courage – a sense of being in control, even in the most terrifying conditions.

Interviewer: Mmm. Which is the most popular risk-taking sport?

David: Oh, probably bungee-jumping. One-and-a-half million people worldwide have tried it. You can jump from a crane, a bridge or a hot-air balloon. You are attached to a length of elastic rope and experience a free fall of nearly one hundred miles an hour before being slowed by an increasing pull on the ankles, which becomes a firm tug as the elastic is pulled tight. Bungee jumpers say there is a moment when they think they'll die and then there's a fantastic rush of adrenalin which hits them like a blinding flash.

Interviewer: Is this what makes people take these extreme risks – the thrill of releasing adrenalin?

David: People's need to experience risk is certainly affected by their physical and psychological make-up. Erm, some individuals, such as extroverts, tend not to get anxious very easily. Other types of people <u>are</u> easily made anxious and tend to avoid sensation. Extroverts are more likely to seek out sensation so they can experience a level of excitement in the body which makes them feel good. They tolerate anxiety or uncertainty better and are more adventurous. Most of us enjoy risk to some extent – we enjoy riding a rollercoaster at theme parks, for example. It's just the degree of risk we will take that counts.

Interviewer: So are you saying you admire the risk-takers more than the dull, stay-at-home type of people?

David: Erm, not exactly. There's obviously a place for both types of people in society. America is said to be the land of the thrill-seeking personality. It was explored by adventurous, strong-willed people who were excited by the unknown. They left their homes to try to create environments which would give them freedom and the chance to prove and develop themselves. In an immigration study, individuals applying for immigration were found to have a higher-than-average level of adventure-seeking traits, which is hardly surprising when you think about it.

Interviewer: Well, you've certainly given us food for thought, David. Thank you for coming into the studio today, and all the best for the book's success.

David: Thank you, Sheila. It's been a pleasure.

Now you will hear the interview again.

That is the end of Part 3, and of the test.

TEST 2, EXTENDED

Part 1, Questions 1 to 6

For questions 1 to 6 you will hear a series of short sentences. Answer each question on the line provided. Your answer should be as brief as possible. You will hear each question twice.

Question 1 You are taking part in an important sports event tomorrow afternoon. What kind of weather can you expect?
Showery weather moving in tonight will make a rather wet start early tomorrow, but this will gradually clear, giving a fine day later.

Question 2 Helga and her brother are talking about buying a birthday present for their father. What sort of present do they decide he would prefer?

Helga: I think Dad would like a book about Formula 1 racing.

Brother: Mmm ... I suppose he <u>might</u> like something like that. But I was wondering about getting him a fishing rod. He's more interested in fishing than car racing these days.

Helga: Yes, that sounds like a good idea.

Question 3 Zoe is ringing to change the time of a job interview. Why does she want to change her interview time? What alternative arrangement does she ask for?

Sales Manager: Bob Baxter, Sales Manager, speaking.

Zoe: Oh hello. My name's Zoe Chamberlain. I've had a letter asking me to come for an interview with you next Monday. I'm afraid I can't come then as I have to take my driving test. Could I have an interview later in the week if possible?

Question 4 Your aunt is expecting a friend to stay with her for a week. Why might the visit have to be postponed?
I've got Dena's room ready for her but she's written to say her brother's very ill. She's not sure she'll be able to come until later in the summer.

Question 5 You need to take some medicine for your cough. What does the doctor advise?
This medicine is helpful in treating cough

symptoms of your sort but you must take it with food. It can cause a nasty stomach upset.

Question 6 You are returning a pair of headphones to the shop. Why will it not be possible for you to get a refund? Give two reasons.
Our policy is very strict with regard to refunds. These headphones have obviously been used several times, so I'm afraid we can't give you your money back. Also, the box they came in has been damaged.

That is the last question in Part 1. In a moment you will hear Part 2. Now look at Part 2, Exercise 1.

Part 2, Exercise 1, Question 7

Listen to this science report about a new way to use solar power, then complete the notes below. You will hear the report twice.

For many people, electricity is a vital part of everyday life and is often taken for granted. But not everyone has access to it. Improving the supply and availability of electricity across the world has challenged scientists for decades. Now, however, technological advances mean that a cheap, safe source of electricity may soon be available virtually anywhere on the planet.

The idea is to harness the sun's energy using satellites. Of course, solar-powered satellites are not a new idea – they were first thought of over thirty years ago, in fact. But it is only relatively recently that technology has advanced far enough to make the idea a practical possibility.

The basic idea is that the solar-powered satellites will convert the energy in sunlight into electricity. The energy will be beamed to earth in the form of microwaves, which will be collected by a device known, quite simply, as a microwave collector. A reconversion plant will then turn the energy harnessed by the microwave collectors into electricity, ready for distribution. The type of solar-powered satellites involved will take just 90 minutes to orbit the earth, and they have many other advantages. These satellites are able to produce electricity extremely efficiently, with less absorption and scattering of radiation.

Developments in technology mean that each solar panel used for harnessing solar energy will be only 200 metres long, and also very light in weight. These advances in solar panels make launching them into orbit much cheaper. As there is no night time in space, it will be possible to generate electricity virtually 24 hours a day.

Scientists are anxious to reassure people about the safety of microwaves. After all, many of us have seen what microwave ovens can do to food, and there are definitely some health issues to consider. However, if the microwaves operate at the correct frequencies, scientists assure us that people and the environment should both be safe.

Now you will hear the report again.

That is the end of Exercise 1. In a moment, you will hear Exercise 2. Now look at the questions for Exercise 2.

Part 2, Exercise 2, Questions 8 to 11

Listen to the interview with a person who works at a falconry centre, then complete the notes below. You will hear the interview twice.

Interviewer: Birds of prey have always been a great source of fascination for adults and children alike. Wildlife Club this week has a special guest, Mike Green from the Dorset Falconry Centre, which has 450 birds of prey including eagles, owls and falcons. Mike, I've heard that there are no fewer than 370 different species of birds of prey worldwide. Is this actually true?

Mike: Yes it is, and whilst many people know that a bird of prey is a hunter and uses its feet to catch food, not many realise that in fact in almost all species the female is the bigger bird.

Interviewer: Really! Now, you've been working at the falconry centre for several years. Why did you become a falconer?

Mike: When I was a child I saw a TV programme about falconry. I was intrigued by the idea of training a bird to fly back to you. The parts of the job which never fail to absorb and challenge me are, I think, understanding how a bird's mind actually works, and then building a relationship of trust with the bird so

I can train it to fly back to me.

Interviewer: It sounds incredible! But how do you actually do it?

Mike: First you get the bird to step on your fist, then jump, and eventually to fly. The trick is to increase the distance that they fly gradually, so that you build up their fitness and stamina. You can get a bird flying within about four days.

Interviewer: Mmm. I can see training the birds must be a very tricky business, requiring a great deal of patience. Now tell me, are the numbers of birds of prey actually increasing?

Mike: Sadly, no. Erm, there's been a huge increase in traffic which has killed off many of them – some simply get knocked down – and then the habitat of many birds has changed and this has had a detrimental effect. However, it's not all gloom. We at the Centre are very into conservation and we have programmes where we breed birds specially for release into the wild. Red kites are one species, for example.

Interviewer: Mmm. Some people say that falconry is cruel and exploits birds. How would you respond?

Mike: Oh, nothing could be further from the truth. We fly all our birds at least once a day, unless they are breeding. What we <u>do</u> think is unfair is when people keep birds of prey at home and try to train them, because it's a very specialist skill. But the Centre does run chidren's training programmes where we let kids handle the birds and teach them about falconry. We also publish a regular newsletter which we send to local schools.

Interviewer: Mmm. Well, thank you very much, Mike, for that very personal insight into falconry, and thank you all for listening.

Now you will hear the interview again.

That is the end of Part 2. In a moment you will hear Part 3. Now look at the questions for Part 3, Exercise 1.

Part 3, Exercise 1, Questions 12 to 18

Listen to the interview with a gardener, then answer the questions in the spaces provided. You will hear the interview twice.

Interviewer: Mariella, you live in a typical London terraced house, with a long thin garden plot at the back, just like all the other houses in the street. But there the similarity ends. Your garden is a – well, I don't know how to describe it – it's a jungle in the nicest possible way, a bit of paradise! You've got hanging baskets bursting with flowers, roses clutch at your feet as you walk along the path. In fact, everywhere you look is bursting with flowering shrubs, bushes and plants of every description at every level! Why did you create the garden?

Mariella: I wanted a garden which would remind me of my native home in Jamaica, although the climate here is very different, of course.

Interviewer: Your father was a farmer, wasn't he? Do your green fingers come from him?

Mariella: No, I haven't got green fingers! No way! My father cultivated bananas for a living but he grew lots of different kinds of vegetables and we lived off what was grown in the garden. And besides vegetables, we had lots of flowers too.

Interviewer: I must say, the exuberance of your garden here certainly captures the atmosphere of a Caribbean landscape. You came here many years ago – it was February, wasn't it?

Mariella: Yes, it was cold and grey when I arrived – not the best time to be here! The garden was nothing but weeds but I saw it and I set to work.

Interviewer: What did you grow at first?

Mariella: My son liked vegetables. He liked to eat them raw, not cooked. So I grew vegetables for him. He would come in from school and munch away at the freshly-picked vegetables: cabbage, carrots, cucumber, pumpkin. I used to get a lot of satisfaction just watching him eat.

Interviewer: How did you learn to garden?

Mariella: I didn't learn from books or anything like that. I would just walk into a shop, see a packet of seeds and plant them, just like that! If they didn't work out, I would keep trying until they did okay. My children weren't interested in the garden but my grandson is keen on gardening. He learned about gardening at school and planted those sunflowers all by himself, although he's only six.

Interviewer: Oh! I couldn't help noticing as we walked through your house the great number of certificates and prizes you've won in gardening competitions. How did you start entering competitions?

Mariella: I was coming home from work one day – I work in a factory across the road – and I saw an old bucket that someone had thrown away. It was in the gutter just outside the factory. I took it home and happened that morning to read an article about a gardening competition. I thought it could make a perfect flower tub. I planted it and took two photos and I got first prize. I was jumping for joy when I found out.

Interviewer: Do you allow yourself a favourite flower?

Mariella: I love the shrimp plant with yellow flowers that is grown in Jamaica. Friends in Jamaica said it would be too cold here for it to flourish, but I planted it in the garden and then took it inside to the living room, where it blooms well.

Interviewer: Have you been back to Jamaica?

Mariella: Several times. On my next trip I'll be taking my two grandchildren with me. I'd like them to experience the freedom of the island. My youngest grandson is mad about mangoes, so I'm going to make him sit under a mango tree and catch a mango as it falls off!

Interviewer: You must derive a great deal of satisfaction from the garden.

Mariella: When I wake up in the morning and look out, you know, it ... it is joy, pure joy.

Now you will hear the interview again.

That is the end of Exercise 1. In a moment you will hear Exercise 2. Now look at the questions for Exercise 2.

Part 3, Exercise 2, Questions 19 to 23

Listen to the interview about how to get the best out of your memory, then answer the questions in the spaces provided. You will hear the interview twice.

Interviewer: Do you have trouble remembering people's names? Do you tend to forget where you put your door key? Then fear not – help is at hand! Today we have with us well-known psychologist Gavin Bonet. Gavin, is there really a way of improving our memories and if so, what are the steps we can take?

Gavin: The first thing to remember is that we can all help ourselves remember effectively by doing quite ordinary things like writing things down, using a diary, a calendar, a notebook, a noticeboard, and checking these things regularly. You can use coloured highlighter pens to pick out really important bits of information. Rather than making your brain lazy, as some people think, scientific studies have proved that these aids encourage a very organised and methodical approach, which helps the brain to function effectively.

Interviewer: Now, I've heard people say, you know, if they want to remember to buy fish for supper they carry around a mental picture of a huge fish flapping on a line. Is there any truth in this? It all sounds a bit strange to me.

Gavin: Centuries ago, the Ancient Greeks developed the system of mnemonics or memory aids. Isolated and fragmented bits of information are very difficult to remember. A mnemonic is a way of linking what you wish to remember with something that means something to you. It could be a mental image, a word, a short poem, and so on. For example, imagine I want to remember the number 1843465. I could link these numbers to personal experiences. 18 is easy – that's the age I went to university, 4 is the number of children I have, 34 is the number of my house and 65 is the age at which I'm going to retire! Linking things we want to remember with rhymes or colours or visual images is helpful as well. Our lifestyle plays a part in memory too. Eating a healthy diet and taking plenty of exercise and having fresh air all help us to be more clear-headed and less absent-minded.

Interviewer: So it's mind and body together, is that it?

Gavin: Yes, I think so. Scientists are gradually finding out more and more about how the brain works and what we can do to assist its functioning. When taking notes, for example, it has been shown that mapping out notes from a central sphere with lines radiating out in different directions is worth adopting because it reflects the way we link information in the brain. Using different coloured pens for note-taking, not just black, helps the brain too.

Interviewer: Are there any differences between men's and women's recall ability, do you think?

Gavin: Ah! Men are good at remembering directions and phone numbers; women are better at names and appointments. Why, we don't really know. You have to take into account upbringing as well as innate differences. Factors that seem to be bad for men and women equally are anxiety and worry. These definitely decrease your thinking ability.

Interviewer: Well, thank you very much, Gavin, for some very interesting and practical suggestions.

Now you will hear the interview again.

That is the end of Part 3, and of the test.

TEST 3, EXTENDED

Part 1, Questions 1 to 6

For questions 1 to 6 you will hear a series of short sentences. Answer each question on the line provided. Your answer should be as brief as possible. You will hear each question twice.

Question 1 Mr Bagir is talking to a group of school leavers about his job as a car mechanic. What kind of experience is most useful when you are training? Whatever kind of training you do, as a trainee car mechanic one thing is very important. You should get experience repairing all kinds of cars.

Question 2 A tourism officer is describing local attractions. What aspect of the area is most popular with tourists?
The town offers festivals and events all year round, there are several historic houses in the area, birdwatching in the nature reserve, and we even have a zoo. But when a survey was carried out last year, we found that the visitors rated the beauty of the countryside above everything else.

Question 3 Ashraf is giving his views on the town he has recently moved to. Why does he like it? Give two reasons.
Before I came, I was told this town was great and it didn't take me long to find out that it's true. People here are so friendly. Everyone says hello to you. Another thing is that I'm so close to the sea. I can walk out of my door and be on the beach in five minutes.

Question 4 Mrs Miller and her family are on their way to have a picnic in a country park. Why will they not be able to have the barbecue they planned?

Mr Miller: Oh no! Did you see that sign over there? It says 'No barbecues due to risk of forest fires', so no hot food for us!

Mrs Miller: Good thing I packed some cheese. We'll just have to eat that with the bread.

Question 5 Juliet is talking about her holiday. What was the best part of the trip?
We had wonderful weather so we did plenty of swimming and sunbathing. But the most memorable bit was the camel ride through the desert – it was brilliant!

Question 6 Louise is ringing up to change a hospital appointment. Why can't she attend? What is she offered instead?

Louise: I've got an appointment with Doctor Brady at 10 o'clock on Thursday morning but I'm taking an exam then. Is it possible to have a different time?

Receptionist: Oh, I see. Erm, thank you for letting us know. I'm afraid Dr Brady's completely booked up this week. Could you come next Monday at 11.30 instead?

That is the last question in Part 1. In a moment you will hear Part 2. Now look at Part 2, Exercise 1.

Part 2, Exercise 1, Question 7

Listen to the report about weather conditions across the world and complete the notes below. You will hear the report twice.

Presenter: Now it's time to move on to our weather slot for an overview of weather conditions across the world last week. Over to you, Mona.

Weatherperson: We've seen some very unusual weather patterns across the world this week, with temperatures fluctuating wildly in places. One of these areas was Denver in the Rockies. The 'mile-high city' saw temperatures soar to 21 degrees Celsius on Monday, 10 degrees above normal for this time of year. In other parts of the United States there were freezing conditions, and snowfalls caused problems across large areas of Canada.

On Tuesday, a tropical storm in Queensland, Australia gave Cairns a deluge of 90 millimetres of rain. By Wednesday, temperatures in Johannesburg, South Africa's largest city, have reached a steamy 35 degrees Celsius, 11 degrees higher than normal for this time of year. Rain has arrived in usually dry locations. On Thursday there was some torrential rain in Algeria, which led to localised flooding. Oman experienced a freak thunderstorm on Friday lasting six hours. Fortunately the tornado which had threatened parts of Central America and was forecast for Saturday did not arrive, but the El Niño effect has brought high winds and rain to many areas of the coastline.

The El Niño weather pattern has also meant continuing drought in south-east Asia, making the forest fires in Indonesia much more severe. Levels of air pollution are increasing, causing concern for those who ...

Now you will hear the report again.

That is the end of Exercise 1. In a moment you will hear Exercise 2. Now look at the questions for Exercise 2.

Part 2, Exercise 2, Questions 8 to 12

Listen to this talk for school leavers who are thinking of taking a year out between school and university. Then complete the notes below. You will hear the talk twice.

Interviewer: Many young people decide to take a year out between leaving school and starting college or university. But is this really such a good idea? With us today we have careers expert Sean Dunne, who has helped many students with these decisions. Sean, what are some of the pros and cons of a year out – or a gap year, as it is sometimes called?

Sean: Well, apart from giving school leavers a break from studying, it's a chance to broaden your horizons and to become a bit more mature before settling down to a university course. However, if you <u>are</u> going to take a year off, think about it in advance – it will affect your future employment. Employers will want you to explain what skills you acquired in the year. So try to choose work which will be useful for your future career. For example, if you're thinking of taking a business studies course, working in an office environment is a good idea. You'll be learning skills such as how to work as part of a team – things you might not have learned at school.

Interviewer: Many students like to travel and see a bit of the world. What would be your advice to them?

Sean: Erm, travelling abroad is very appealing, of course, but make sure you know what's involved. You should research the countries you want to visit carefully, and find out about health requirements, visas and the cost of living.

Interviewer: What about actually working abroad? Is it a good idea and, if so, how should you go about it?

Sean: Finding a job abroad can certainly help you financially. In my view, it's best to arrange employment before you go. One good way is by contacting an agency – make sure it's reputable, of course! Popular jobs for students are working on farms, in holiday camps or for families. Just a word of warning, though: if you do go abroad, make sure you're not away when you need to attend interviews in your home country.

Interviewer: So, be at home when needed for your university or college interview!

Sean: Yes. And I'd like to say to those students who may be listening and like the idea of travel – by all means follow up any suitable opportunity, but don't expect it to be an easy option.

Interviewer: Thank you, Sean. Well, that's it for today. Next week we'll be talking about ...

Now you will hear the talk again.

That is the end of Part 2. In a moment you will hear Part 3. Now look at the questions for Part 3, Exercise 1.

Part 3, Exercise 1, Questions 13 to 19

Listen to this interview with an archaeologist and answer the questions in the spaces provided. You will hear the interview twice.

Interviewer: Today I'm visiting someone who spends his working day digging amongst the ruins and tombs of ancient Egypt. Tony, what is it like being an archaeologist?

Tony: Hot and dusty! At the moment I'm working at a site in the Valley of the Kings. We're exploring a royal burial site and have reached the innermost part of the underground tombs. As soon as we arrive in the morning, we're given all the equipment we're going to need for going underground: dust masks, because the dust is so bad, er, trowels and picks. Everything has been slower than we'd hoped, but you get used to the frustrations of this kind of project.

Interviewer: It sounds a bit like being a miner – not exactly glamorous! What appeals to you about it?

Tony: Well, er, it's not the salary or the working conditions! But there's always the exciting possibility of discovering something wonderful – especially here in Egypt. You learn to listen for the sound of metal hitting stone. This indicates that an artefact may be buried beneath the dirt and dust. The hope of finding something wonderful makes it all worthwhile.

Interviewer: What time do you actually start work?

Tony: Very early. Erm, we've been leaving the hotel before dawn and taking a ferry ride across the Nile. We had a good day yesterday, as we dug up a red granite block that was buried in one of the tombs. When we had brushed away the dirt and dust, we saw strange figures and markings on it. I made out the name of a king's daughter – we already know about her. But we also discovered the name of another woman – we don't yet know who she was. She may have been a queen and, if so, I wonder why we hadn't heard of her before.

Interviewer: Ah, in other words, you've got a mystery lady on your hands.

Tony: Yes! We know she must have been important to have been buried in a marble and granite tomb. We actually found further fragments of granite which may provide some clues to her identity.

Interviewer: Are there many tourists around?

Tony: There's usually a small crowd of visitors at the site, eager to see what's being brought to the surface. They stay behind a roped area.

Interviewer: Do you spend the whole of your working day digging and sorting finds?

Tony: No. Er, we usually dig until around 1 o'clock, and then, after a shower and lunch, I often meet fellow archaeologists at the library. Erm, we use this time to go through reference books, checking for information about things we've found.

Interviewer: Ah. And what do you do in the evenings?

Tony: It varies. Erm, tonight I'm going to visit the Luxor temple. The walls of the temple are lit by electric light, so I'll be able to read the inscriptions on them. I'll be looking for clues to the identity of the lady named on the block we found.

Interviewer: What are your plans for the future?

Tony: Well, various projects have been suggested. Erm, I could make a documentary or radio programme about the Valley of the Kings, but I don't like the way the media treat the topic – they tend to sensationalise it. My preferred choice is to write a book about ancient Egypt. It will be for anyone who is interested – the general reader. It won't be aimed at experts in the field.

Interviewer: It sounds fascinating, Tony. And the very best of luck with it.

Tony: Thank you.

Now you will hear the interview again.

That is the end of Exercise 1. In a moment you will hear Exercise 2. Now look at the questions for Exercise 2.

Part 3, Exercise 2, Questions 20 to 25

Listen to this talk about closed circuit television and answer the questions in the spaces provided. You will hear the talk twice.

Do you ever feel you're being watched? Well, you probably are! There are around 300,000 closed circuit television cameras in the UK alone, and it's estimated that you have a very good chance of appearing on a TV screen. CCTV, as it's known, is designed to cut crime, but does it also invade our privacy?

Special cameras in public places send pictures straight to TV screens, where they're monitored and taped. You can be watched in many places – shopping centres, car parks, supermarkets, cashpoints, railway stations and offices. CCTV can be small scale – just one camera and a TV screen in a food shop, for instance. Or it may be a network of cameras covering a large area like an airport, monitored in a control room by trained security staff, often in contact with the police.

CCTV has been around since the 1970s, but it has only become widespread since about 1990. However, the idea of filming people to prevent crime goes back much further. In 1824 a pickpocket was seen in action by a camera obscura, which was an early type of camera, at a fair in Scotland. Somebody suggested at the time that camera obscuras should be used by the police to observe the streets and catch criminals, but people didn't believe this could work.

CCTV has been shown to help reduce crime. There's been a reduction in crimes such as theft and vandalism in areas which are covered by CCTV systems. But it seems that criminals don't <u>stop</u> committing crimes – they just commit them somewhere that doesn't <u>have</u> CCTV. This is called displacement crime. Recent research shows that installing CCTV cameras in main streets increases the fear of crime in side streets, where there is <u>no</u> coverage.

Some people say that if you don't break the law, you have nothing to worry about from CCTV. But I think many ordinary people are against CCTV because of the invasion of their privacy. In my view, people see the need for privacy as very important and don't like the idea of being watched whilst on normal everyday business.

At the moment there are no laws in the UK controlling who sets up CCTV or what happens to the tapes. There are only voluntary guidelines. This means there is potential for the system to be abused. You could find a tape of yourself at a shopping centre being used in a quite different context. I feel strongly that images of a person should have the same protection as written information about them, and CCTV tapes should only be used for crime prevention.

Now you will hear the talk again

That is the end of Part 3, and of the test.

TEST 4, EXTENDED

Part 1, Questions 1 to 6

For questions 1 to 6 you will hear a series of short sentences. Answer each question on the line provided. Your answer should be as brief as possible. You will hear each question twice.

Question 1 Iveta is confirming arrangements for a flight to America. Which item does the travel agent remind her to bring?
Your flight leaves at 10.30 a.m. You'll need to check in two hours before departure. Your tickets and visa will be ready for collection at the desk. Don't forget your passport, will you? That's the most important thing.

Question 2 Aysha and Peter would like to go swimming after school. How will they get to the swimming pool?

Aysha: I suppose we could walk or cycle to the pool – it's not that far.

Peter: Yes, but it's so hot we'll be exhausted by the time we get there. How about getting a number 38 bus? It stops right outside.

Aysha: That's a good idea. And we could use our bus passes.

Question 3 You are at a meeting about recycling in your neighbourhood. Where does the speaker want to put the recycling bins? How often does he think the collection should be carrried out?
People around here are living at breakneck speed and don't want to recycle absolutely everything. I think the new twice-weekly collection targets are quite unrealistic. Once a week is perfectly all right. And we need to move the recycling bins to the supermarket car park – having them at the entrance to the store is very inconvenient.

Question 4 Martha is inviting a visitor to her country to a festival. What is the festival celebrating?
Have you heard about the festival in the market place on Saturday? Everyone is going to dress up in historical costumes to celebrate one hundred years of independence. It sounds great. Would you like to come with us?

Question 5 You hear this information on local radio. What website address do they recommend?
And finally, for explanations in simple English about how hundreds of things work, from car engines to the internet, don't miss this extremely useful website: www.howstuffworks.com. That's our tip for the week. More next Tuesday.

Question 6 Mrs Taylor is ringing a friend to ask a favour. What does John need? Why?
Sorry to trouble you, Eileen, but could you possibly call for John on your way to work and give him a lift to school? He hurt his leg playing basketball at the weekend. The nurse who bandaged it said he was very lucky not to have broken it.

That is the last question in Part 1. In a moment you will hear Part 2. Now look at Part 2, Exercise 1.

Part 2, Exercise 1, Questions 7 to 11

Listen to this local radio announcement about a forthcoming 'fun run' and complete the notes below. You will hear the announcement twice.

The tenth annual Community Fun Run, which takes athletes around the streets and parks of our town, will be held next Saturday. This year a total of 130 entrants will be taking part, from local schools, offices, factories, colleges and hospitals. Entrants will be raising money for charities of their choice. Athletes, whose ages range from eight to eighty, are busy doing some last-minute training before the big day. Here are details of just a few of them.

Laura Corville from St Mary's High School has run in two previous fun runs and will be eighteen on the day of the race. She is hoping to raise several hundred pounds for new scanning equipment at the district hospital.

Other participants are newer to the 'running for charity' scene. May Ayad from the village of Drayton has run only once before. She is hoping to beat her last year's time of 44 minutes 19 seconds and to raise money for Guide Dogs for the Blind. May told us she gets up early each day and runs for at least half an hour before starting work. Thomas Meyer is from Germany and studying computer science at the university. He will be taking part this year for the first time. Thomas is raising money for the Endangered Wildlife Research Fund. He told reporters that running the race was the most exciting event of his year.

The race starts at 10 a.m. at Hillfield Park and finishes at the Performing Arts Centre, where prizes will be awarded according to age group. A First Aid service will be located on the corner of Driver's Avenue and Sandy Lane, and will be staffed by volunteers with medical training. If you are keen on competing in the Fun Run, we would like to hear from you.

Now you will hear the announcement again.

That is the end of Exercise 1. In a moment you will hear Exercise 2. Now look at Exercise 2.

Part 2, Exercise 2, Question 12

Listen to the radio interview about human survival and complete the notes below. You will hear the interview twice.

Interviewer: Hello and welcome to Saturday Science. Today we're going to hear from Professor Vicki Karidis, who lectures in Natural Sciences at the University of Perth. Professor Karidis, people live in the Sahara Desert, where temperatures reach 50 degrees Celsius – hot enough, so I'm told, to fry an egg – and also in Siberia, where temperatures can be as low as minus 65 degrees Celsius, which is much colder than my freezer! How is it possible for the human body to survive such extremes?

Professor: Well, a number of factors are involved. Firstly, different physical characteristics – skin and eye colour, body shape and so on – have evolved in different parts of the world over long periods of time. Secondly, and perhaps more importantly, every human being is naturally able to adapt. For example, we are all able to sweat when we feel hot, which is the body's way of releasing salt and water in order to keep us cool. We are also able to shiver when we feel cold, which is the body's way of increasing heat production. In very cold temperatures, the human body will also quite naturally cut down on heat loss. Finally, we have developed skills and lifestyles which enable us to build the right kinds of shelter, eat appropriate foods and wear clothing which protects us and is suitable for the kind of environment we live in.

Interviewer: Is it easier to survive heat rather than cold?

Professor: Yes, it is. Scientists believe that fossils found in Africa are evidence that human life began in that part of the world. Our ancestors could cope quite naturally with the heat. When people began to travel and settle in cooler parts of the world, they took the ability to adapt to heat with them. People who live in cold climates, like the Inuit, the native people of Greenland, have developed a natural ability to cope with the extreme cold. For example, Inuit hunters can grip their harpoons in temperatures that would cause other people's fingers to go numb. Without this ability to hunt and get food, they wouldn't survive the extreme climate.

Interviewer: Mmm. How do people who live at very high altitudes manage to survive? Is it a case of getting used to the environment?

Professor: People who live at high altitudes – in the Andes for example – have adapted to reduced levels of oxygen. Air at high altitudes is much thinner, and this can be very uncomfortable for someone used to living near sea level. The first sign of altitude sickness is a headache, and at very high altitudes the condition can be fatal.

Interviewer: Ah! Although people have adapted to live in various climates, we still need special equipment if we're to survive underwater. Is this likely to be something we can overcome?

Professor: As you say, we are still dependent on breathing apparatus if we want to go underwater for any length of time. Going underwater puts great pressure on our lungs. At a depth of 10 metres, pressure on the lungs doubles. However, Japanese divers searching for pearls can dive as deep as 20 metres without special breathing equipment. They have developed natural breathing techniques to expand their lung capacity, enabling them to stay underwater for longer. So, perhaps other people will be able to do this too, in time. The human body has an amazing ...

Now you will hear the interview again.

That is the end of Part 2. In a moment you will hear Part 3. Now look at the questions for Part 3, Exercise 1.

Part 3, Exercise 1, Questions 13 to 17

Listen to this interview with a schoolboy who acts in a television series and answer the questions in the spaces provided. You will hear the interview twice.

Interviewer: Now it's time for our regular weekly slot where we talk to young people who are achieving something unusual with their lives. This week we have teenage pop musician and TV star Julian Hendry with us in the studio.

Julian, you've been appearing in a TV series called The Star Game, in which you play a teenager who starts a pop group with some friends. The series has been a huge success. Can you tell our listeners how it all started?

Julian: Well, I won an award in a music competition in my home town, Brigton, and the local newspaper did an article about me. By coincidence the producer of The Star Game was looking for someone about my age to take part in the series. He had already signed up three other teenagers for parts in the show and needed a fourth. He got in touch through the newspaper. Er, I did a couple of auditions where I had to sing, play my guitar and read aloud, and then I was offered the part. It all happened so quickly! I didn't really have time to think about it.

Interviewer: Hm! What was being filmed like?

Julian: Well, we were told to pretend that the camera wasn't there. It seemed strange at first, but after a while I did get used to it. Acting was more difficult than I expected, but the director gave me lots of advice during the rehearsal about how to develop the character and how to say my lines. We got to know all the camera crew really well, and they had a big party for us when we finished filming the series.

Interviewer: How did you get on with the other actors?

Julian: Er, very well, mostly, but I think there was a bit of rivalry between Alex Garcia and me. Er, we've got very similar musical styles and we both want to produce the same kinds of records.

Interviewer: Hm, hm. Have you always wanted to be a pop star?

Julian: Er, as a child I dreamed of being a professional footballer but I didn't have the skills and was never talent spotted. I'm a fan of my home team, though, Brigton United, and travel all over the country to watch them play. I'm playing for my school team this weekend in a match with another school, and after that we're all going round to a friend's house to watch football videos. I'd like to make it as a pop star in the future, but even if I don't, I'd like to stay in the music business. I love music magazines, so maybe writing articles for a music magazine would be pretty good too.

Interviewer: What kind of music do you listen to?

Julian: Er, it depends on my mood and what I'm doing. I listen to a bit of classical music when I'm doing my homework, otherwise it's pop or soul. I find music really helps me relax, and I play it most of the time.

Interviewer: How has appearing on TV affected your schoolwork?

Julian: It's all right at the moment because we've finished the first series, but when I start the next series it's going to be hard. I've got my GCSEs coming up, and my parents think I should put studying first.

Interviewer: Mmm. Do you have any musical training?

Julian: Hm, hm. I had to learn the piano when I was little but I hated it. Then when I was about thirteen I got together with a group of school friends and we formed our own band. I played the guitar and sang and did a bit of drumming. We also wrote our own songs. Now my younger brother Kevin is also keen to start a band, so I'm giving him some guitar coaching.

Interviewer: Hmm. What do you think is the secret of becoming successful?

Julian: Mmm. Er, hard work and focus. You've really got to concentrate, and also to imagine yourself picking up a big award for the work you do.

Now you will hear the interview again.

That is the end of Exercise 1. In a moment you will hear Exercise 2. Now look at the questions for Exercise 2.

Part 3, Exercise 2, Questions 18 to 24

Listen to this talk about children's health given by a doctor and answer the questions in the spaces provided. You will hear the talk twice.

Good morning and welcome everyone, and thank you all for coming along this morning. My name is Clare Harvey, and my talk today is based on my latest book, 'Children's Health in the Modern World'. The book was the result of many years' research into children's needs across a wide age range, from babyhood through to the teenage years.

As a doctor, I was not satisfied with simply treating the physical symptoms of illness, and I began to be more and more convinced that social and other factors were terribly important in children's health. As I mentioned, the book is the result of many years work in this field, and I hope it will help the general public to be more aware of the social and psychological factors which affect children's health.

In my work as a doctor I often see children who have not returned to good health even though the physical symptoms of the illness which I have treated them for may have gone. They say they feel low and depressed, they're not doing well at school, or they're not getting on with the rest of the family. I'm often asked about the causes of these problems. And I have to say there is no one definite cause, and no particular rules we can observe, as problems affect children from all classes and backgrounds. Take moving house, for example. One child might be very upset by the move and take a lot of time to settle down, whilst another finds it very easy and quickly makes new friends. How they cope with a change of environment is to do with their individual natures as much as anything.

If a child does come to me – and I see some as young as six or seven – and they don't want to get out of bed in the morning, I tell parents or teachers that it is very important to listen, as this may be a cry for help, and to try to find the reasons for this behaviour. I think children in the modern world are often coping with more pressures than I had as a child. Their parents may have insecure employment and be worried about losing their jobs, or parents may have less time because they are both going out to work, and so on. School can be a source of great stress too – there is more emphasis on achievement and getting high marks.

What I have noticed is a difference between boys and girls. I see more girls than boys in my clinic, without doubt, as girls will generally share their problems more readily and quickly than boys. I think it is wrong to see children as helpless victims who can do nothing for themselves. What I think we must realise is that children can be very resourceful and do things for themselves, and it is essential that this resourcefulness is encouraged. Children have rights and needs as much as anyone else. We should not put labels on them, and any discussion about the best way we can ...

Now you will hear the talk again

That is the end of Part 3, and of the test.

KEY

TEST 1, CORE

Part 1

1 too tight
2 aimed at children, not teenagers/aimed at children/not for his age group
3 borrow some CDs

4 check whether/if history book ready for collection
5 not a sign of illness
6 **(i)** don't dive in
   (ii) too shallow/might hit head on bottom

Part 2, Exercise 1

7 *See below.*

PERSONAL SAFETY

If you are visiting a place for the first time make sure you ...... **know the route** ...... and the exact address of where you are going. Always .... **tell your parents where you are going** ...., including the arrangements for .... **the return journey** ....

When you use a bus by yourself, choose a seat ...... **close to the driver** .... If you are walking late at night, keep to well-lit streets and avoid crossing ...... **parks** ...... or waste ground or going down dark alleys. If you are lost, ask a policeman for directions or ...... **go into a shop** ...... for help. Keep your purse or wallet out of sight at all times.

To keep your home safe from burglary, never ...... **write your address on** ...... your door key or leave it under a flowerpot or doormat. At night, it's a good idea to ...... **draw your curtains** .... Don't leave money or expensive jewellery where they can easily be seen ...... **through the window** .... Get to ...... **know your neighbours** ...... and if you are concerned about a stranger in the area, tell the police. On the telephone, do not ...... **give your name** ...... to an unknown caller if you are at home alone.

Finally, ... **gates and window locks** ...... can further protect your home, so discuss this with your parents if you feel such measures would be helpful. Remember, however, that serious crime is very rare indeed.

Part 2, Exercise 2

 8 **(a)** physical fitness programme
 9 **(a)** new drugs
10 **(b)** put space research on curriculum
11 more pupils are considering a career in science
12 scientists can communicate well/better
13 the whole world would benefit

Part 3, Exercise 1

14 **(a)** T **(b)** F **(c)** T **(d)** F **(e)** T **(f)** F
    (g) T **(h)** F **(i)** T **(j)** T **(k)** F **(l)** F

Part 3, Exercise 2

15 D 16 D 17 B 18 C 19 B

TEST 2, CORE

Part 1

1 room 12
2 Monday 6th August
3 no photograph

4 friend's brother ill
5 take it with food
6 **(i)** have been damaged
  (ii) box damaged

Part 2, Exercise 1

7 *See below.*

SOLAR POWER FOR EVERYONE

Advances in technology mean that a cheap, ...*safe*............... source of electricity may soon be available worldwide.

Solar-powered satellites will change sunlight into electricity. The energy will be beamed to earth by microwaves, to be collected by a .....*microwave*........... ......*collector*........... .

Advantages of solar-powered satellites:
• **Take only 90 minutes to orbit earth.**
• *Produce electricity very* ....*efficiently*............... .
• **Less scattering and absorption of radiation.**

Advances in technology now mean that solar panels will be only 200 metres long and also ....*very light in weight*............... , which will make launching them into space ....*much cheaper*............... .

Scientists believe that if the ......*microwaves operate*............... at the correct frequencies, people and the environment will both be safe.

Part 2, Exercise 2

8 **(iii)** female is bigger
9 **(i)** understanding how a bird's mind works
10 **(i)** increase in traffic
  (ii) habitat has changed
  (iii) for release into the wild
11 **(i)** runs training programmes

Part 3, Exercise 1

12 **(a)** T **(b)** T **(c)** F **(d)** T **(e)** F **(f)** T
  (g) F **(h)** F **(i)** F **(j)** T **(k)** F **(l)** T

Part 3, Exercise 2

13 D **14** B **15** A **16** C **17** B

TEST 3, CORE

Part 1

1 6.45
2 business studies

3 training for a competition
4 risk of forest fires/not allowed
5 camel ride through desert
6 **(i)** exam
  (ii) Monday 11.30

Part 2, Exercise 1

7

The weather last week

Weather in general: Great fluctuations in temperatures.

Monday

Denver, Rockies: 21°C, 10 degrees above normal. ......**Freezing**...... conditions in other places in U.S. and ......**snowfalls**...... in Canada. [1]

Tuesday

Cairns, Queensland: ......**tropical storm**...... with 90 mm rain. [1]

Wednesday

Johannesburg: ......**35**...... °C, ...**11**...... degrees above normal. [1]

Thursday

Algeria: torrential rain, some floods.

Friday

Oman: freak ......**thunderstorm**...... lasting 6 hours. [1]

Saturday

Central America: ......**tornado**...... did not arrive but El Niño effect brought ......**high winds**...... and ......**rain**...... to many areas of the coastline. [1]

Also caused by El Niño

Continuing drought in S.E.Asia.

Indonesia: *forest fires* much worse and increased levels of *air pollution*.

Part 2, Exercise 2

8 (c) become more mature
9 (a) what skills you acquired
  (b) work which will be useful in future career
10 (a) health requirements
  (b) visas
  (c) cost of living

11 (b) farms, holiday camps, families

Part 3, Exercise 1

12 B **13** C **14** A **15** C **16** B

Part 3, Exercise 2

17 The true statements are: b, d, e, f, h, j

Test 4, Core

Part 1

1 gym
2 lost property box
3 washing powder
4 100 years of independence
5 www.howstuffworks.com.

6 (i) lift to school
  (ii) hurt leg playing basketball

Part 2, Exercise 1

7 Saturday; 130
8 18; scanning equipment
9 44 minutes 19 seconds; Guide Dogs for the Blind
10 Germany; computer science

11

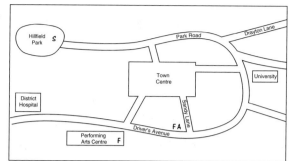

Part 3, Exercise 1

13 The true statements are: a, b, d, g, h, k

Part 3, Exercise 2

14 C **15** B **16** A **17** C **18** A

Part 2, Exercise 2

12

Surviving Extremes

The human body can survive extremes of climate because

- physical characteristics have evolved over time

- every human being is able to ......**adapt**.............. [1]

E.g. we can ......**sweat**.................. when it is hot, we can *shiver* when it is cold,

and we can also cut down on heat loss from the body. [1]

- We have developed ......**skills**................ and ......**lifestyles**............ which enable

  us to build suitable shelter, eat the right food and have protective clothing. [1]

Scientists believe that fossils found in Africa show that *human life began* there.

When people moved to cooler areas they took ......**the ability to adapt**...............

with them. [1]

At high altitudes, people have adapted to *reduced levels of oxygen*.

A headache is the ...**first sign of altitude sickness**............................ [1]

Special equipment still needed to survive, because of pressure on lungs.

Japanese pearl divers have developed ......**natural breathing techniques**....

to allow them to stay underwater for longer. [1]

Test 1, Extended

Part 1

1 problems in engine
2 camping

3 (i) children throwing stones at dog
   (ii) report to police
4 check whether/if history book ready for collection
5 not a sign of illness
6 (i) don't dive in
   (ii) too shallow/might hit head on bottom

Part 2, Exercise 1

7

PERSONAL SAFETY

If you are visiting a place for the first time make sure you .....**know the route**................................

and the exact address of where you are going. Always ....**tell your parents where you**...........

.....**are going**.............., including the arrangements for ....**the return journey**....................... .

When you use a bus by yourself, choose a seat ....**close to the driver**..................... . If you are

walking late at night, keep to well-lit streets and avoid crossing ....**parks**..................................

or waste ground or going down dark alleys. If you are lost, ask a policeman for directions or

......**go into a shop**................................ for help. Keep your purse or wallet out of sight at all times.

To keep your home safe from burglary, never ......**write your address on**...................................

your door key or leave it under a flowerpot or doormat. At night, it's a good idea to

......**draw your curtains**......................... . Don't leave money or expensive jewellery where they

can easily be seen ......**through the window**... . Get to

.......**know your neighbours**.................... and if you are concerned about a stranger in the area,

tell the police. On the telephone, do not ......**give your name**................................ to an unknown

caller if you are at home alone.

Finally, ...**gates and window locks**........................... can further protect your home, so discuss

this with your parents if you feel such measures would be helpful. Remember, however, that serious

crime is very rare indeed.

Part 2, Exercise 2

8 (a) physical fitness programme
   (c) learning about technical aspects of space travel/ learning to operate the spacecraft/learning to use all the systems
9 (a) new drugs
   (b) developments in electronics
10 (a) make science more exciting
   (b) put space research on the curriculum
11 more pupils are considering a career in science
12 scientists can communicate well/better
13 the whole world would benefit

Part 3, Exercise 1

14 *Any 2 of:* access in remote areas/diagnosis and treatment can be given immediately/ access to best doctors

15 can be monitored at a distance
16 can watch (famous) surgeon perform techniques
17 can get clues from appearance/face/ expression/dress/mannerisms
18 helped patients understand their problems

Part 3, Exercise 2

19 World has eliminated risk/We want to guarantee safety/emphasis on safety
20 They need excitement/find normal life too dull
21 *Any 2 of:* help them overcome fears/learn to stay in control/help them develop courage
22 They get anxious easily/are easily made anxious
23 There is a place in society for both types
24 adventure-seeking/adventurous people

TEST 2, EXTENDED

Part 1

1 fine weather
2 fishing rod
3 **(i)** driving test
  (ii) later in week

4 friend's brother ill
5 take it with food
6 **(i)** have been used
  (ii) box damaged

Part 2, Exercise 1

7 *See below.*

SOLAR POWER FOR EVERYONE

Advances in technology mean that a cheap, ...*safe*...... source of electricity may soon be available worldwide.

Solar-powered satellites will change sunlight into electricity. The energy will be beamed to earth by microwaves, to be collected by a .....*microwave* ......*collector*...... .

Advantages of solar-powered satellites:

• Take only 90 minutes to orbit earth.
• ......*Produce electricity very efficiently*...... .
• Less scattering and absorption of radiation.

Advances in technology now mean that solar panels will be only 200 metres long and also ......*very light in weight*......, which will make launching them into space ......*much cheaper*...... .

Scientists believe that if the ......*microwaves operate*...... at the correct frequencies, people and the environment will both be safe.

Part 2, Exercise 2

8 **(i)** 370
  (iii) female is bigger
9 **(i)** understanding how a bird's mind works
  (ii) building a relationship of trust
10 **(i)** increase in traffic
   (ii) habitat has changed
   (iii) for release into the wild
11 **(i)** runs training programmes
   (ii) sends newsletter to schools

Part 3, Exercise 1

12 similar to other houses but garden is different (like a jungle)
13 farmer/grew bananas
14 Her son liked them/liked raw vegetables
15 would keep trying/would try again
16 noticed certificates and prizes (in the house)
17 **(i)** found an old bucket/a suitable container/a suitable tub (outside factory)
   (ii) read an article about it
18 to experience the freedom of the island

Part 3, Exercise 2

19 Scientific studies/research shows that they help the brain/that the brain benefits from an organised/methodical approach

20 doubtful/thinks it sounds strange/finds it hard to believe

21 *Any 2 of:* diet, exercise, fresh air
22 reflects the way we link information in the brain
23 anxiety/worry

TEST 3, EXTENDED

Part 1

1 repairing all kinds of cars
2 beauty of the countryside
3 **(i)** people are friendly
  (ii) close to the sea

4 risk of forest fires/not allowed
5 camel ride through desert
6 **(i)** exam
  (ii) Monday 11.30

Part 2, Exercise 1

7 *See below.*

The weather last week

Weather in general: Great fluctuations in temperatures.

Monday

Denver, Rockies: 21°C, 10 degrees above normal. ....**Freezing**......... conditions in

other places in U.S. and ....**snowfalls**............... in Canada.   [1]

Tuesday

Cairns, Queensland: ....**tropical storm**........ with 90 mm rain.   [1]

Wednesday

Johannesburg: ....**35**....... °C, ...**11**.............. degrees above normal.   [1]

Thursday

Algeria: torrential rain, some floods.

Friday

Oman: freak ....**thunderstorm**......... lasting 6 hours.   [1]

Saturday

Central America: .....**tornado**........ did not arrive but El Niño effect brought

........**high winds**........ and ....**rain**........... to many areas of the coastline.   [1]

Also caused by El Niño

Continuing drought in S.E.Asia.

Indonesia: ....**forest fires**............... much worse and increased levels of

.......**air pollution**................ .   [1]

Part 2, Exercise 2

8 **(b)** broaden your horizons
   (c) become more mature
9 **(a)** what skills you acquired
   (b) work which will be useful in your future career
10 **(a)** health requirements
   (b) visas
   (c) cost of living
11 **(a)** contacting an agency
   (b) farms, holiday camps, families
12 are not away when you need to go/attend

Part 3, Exercise 1

13 Valley of the Kings (in Egypt)
14 possibility/chance of discovering something wonderful
15 name of an unknown woman/a queen/an important woman/a mystery woman

16 meets other archaeologists in library/checks things (in reference books) in library
17 to look for clues about the unknown woman
18 thinks they don't treat the subject seriously/they sensationalise the subject
19 write a book about ancient Egypt (for the general public)

Part 3, Exercise 2

20 There are so many/300,000 CCTV cameras in the UK
21 one camera and one screen in food shop
22 since 1990
23 People didn't think/believe it could work
24 They commit crimes somewhere else/ elsewhere
25 invasion of privacy

TEST 4, EXTENDED

Part 1

1 passport
2 by bus
3 **(i)** supermarket car park
   (ii) once a week
4 100 years of independence
5 www.howstuffworks.com
6 **(i)** lift to school
   (ii) hurt leg playing basketball

Part 2, Exercise 1

7 Saturday; 130
8 18; new scanning equipment
9 44 minutes 19 seconds; Guide Dogs for the Blind
10 Germany; computer science
11

Part 2, Exercise 2

12

Surviving Extremes

The human body can survive extremes of climate because

*   physical characteristics have evolved over time
*   every human being is able to ......**adapt**...................... [1]

E.g. we can ......**sweat**................... when it is hot, we can .....**shiver**....... when it is

cold, and we can also cut down on heat loss from the body. [2]

*   We have developed ......**skills**........................ and ......**lifestyles**.................. which enable

    us to build suitable shelter, eat the right food and have protective clothing. [1]

Scientists believe that fossils found in Africa show that ....**human life**...........

........**began**................... there. [1]

When people moved to cooler areas they took ....**the ability to adapt**................

with them. [1]

At high altitudes, people have adapted to ....**reduced levels of oxygen**........ [1]

A headache is the ....**first sign of altitude sickness**................ [1]

Special equipment still needed to survive, because of pressure on lungs. [1]

Japanese pearl divers have developed ....**natural breathing techniques**....

to allow them to stay underwater for longer. [1]

Part 3, Exercise 1

13 He won an award/won a music competition
14 (i) how to develop the character
    (ii) how to say lines
15 play football for school team/go to friend's house/watch football videos
16 wrote songs for own pop band
17 He wants to start a band

Part 3, Exercise 2

18 make people aware of social and psychological factors (in children's health)

19 *Any 1 of:* feel low/feel depressed/not doing well at school/not getting on with family
20 individual/different natures
21 should listen to children/try to find reasons for behaviour
22 *Any 1 of:* more pressures/parents have insecure employment/parents have less time/ more emphasis on achievement (at school)/more emphasis on high marks
23 Girls share problems (more readily/quickly)
24 We should encourage their resourcefulness

ORAL EXAMINER'S NOTES

The following notes are for guidance on the development phase only of each discussion. See pages 12–13 of the Introduction for step-by-step instructions on running a mock Oral Assessment, including the warm-up and preparation phases.

A Homecoming Party: Candidate's Notes

One of your relatives is shortly going to return home after several years overseas. You would like to plan a party for him/her. Discuss with your partner or the Examiner what you will do to make sure the party is a complete success. The following may give you some ideas:

- who to invite
- where to have the party
- music and decorations
- whether to tell your relative about the party or keep it as a surprise
- food and drink.

Development
Allow the candidate(s) to talk about the idea of a homecoming celebration and why this kind of party is more or less likely to be a success than an ordinary party. Encourage them to discuss the pros and cons of parties including: ways to create a good atmosphere, the chances of damage occurring, why some people hate parties, keeping to a party budget, dressing for parties.

Extended level candidates
Lead the candidates on to discuss other aspects of 'homecoming' for someone who has been away for several years, including: the possible stresses of adapting to the old way of life, how he/she may have changed, other things the candidate could do to make the person returning feel welcomed and valued.

B A Memorial: Candidate's Notes

Your town is planning to erect a memorial of some kind to an important person who has died in recent years. Local people have been asked to put forward their views about the kind of memorial they would like. Discuss with your partner or the Examiner the person you would erect a memorial to and the sort of memorial you would like to see. You may like to consider such ideas as:

- the person who deserves to be remembered in this way and why
- the kind of memorial you would like to see
- the best ways of raising funds to build the memorial.

Development
Encourage the candidate(s) to describe a person they admire and to explain aspects of their achievements, personal skills, qualities, etc which they feel have contributed to society and should be remembered. Ask candidates to explain the sort of memorial they would choose, and why they feel it is more appropriate than other kinds. Encourage them to speculate about the best ways to involve the community in raising funds to develop the memorial. Invite them to talk about any actual memorials they have visited, their own feelings about them, and the effect the memorial has on the surrounding landscape and community.

Extended level candidates

Lead the candidates on to discuss whether problems could arise, such as disputes over the best kind of memorial, possible graffiti or vandalism, preserving the memorial well, and ways of promoting it to the wide range of people who may wish to visit it. They could discuss whether scholarships or trust funds make better memorials than physical objects.

C Rules at Home: Candidate's Notes

Most families have rules of some kind. Discuss with your partner or the Examiner your views about rules at home. You may wish to consider such things as:

- typical rules
- whether rules improve family life and, if so, why or why not
- suitable punishments – if any – for people who break the rules
- why some families have more behaviour problems than others
- whether TV and computer games have a bad effect on family behaviour.

Development

Discuss with the candidate(s) the points raised. In particular, allow them to describe rules which work well in their own experience and those which do not. Allow them to talk about rules which they particularly dislike and to explain why. Invite them to suggest ways they would change family life to avoid the need for certain rules, if they could.

Extended level candidates

Lead the discussion on to a more detailed examination of rules in society. This could lead on to an exploration of the reasons for crime and what can be done to reduce crime, both in the candidates' own neighbourhood and in the wider society.

D Staying Safe: Candidate's Notes

Young children have to learn about safety and ways to avoid placing themselves in dangerous situations. Discuss with your partner or the Examiner ways children can avoid coming to harm. You may use the ideas below, but you are also free to make up ideas of your own.

- problems associated with traffic
- dangers in the home
- dangers associated with playing outside the home
- dangers at school.

Development

Discuss with the candidate(s) the ideas put forward. Encourage them to talk about any personal experiences they had of safety problems when younger, or any observations they have made from observing safety problems among young children living near them. In particular they could be asked to explore a specific topic such as safety in the home or at school, and asked what measures could be taken to make these environments as safe as possible.

Extended level candidates

Lead the candidates on to discuss whether the world is less safe for young children than it used to be and, if so, why. The implications of restrictions on young children intended to keep them safe could be explored, such as whether such restrictions lead to a loss of freedom and independence, with negative consequences for child development.

E Training for Jobs or Better Health?: Candidate's Notes

Your town has a limited budget and has to decide whether to close either a training centre or a clinic. The training centre trains unemployed people in skills to help them find jobs; the clinic treats minor illnesses and injuries and carries out small operations. The town has asked local people which they think should close. Discuss your own views with your partner of the Examiner.

Development

Discuss with the candidate(s) the points raised. Areas to consider might be: the severity of unemployment in the neighbourhood, alternative job training arrangements that could be offered, ease of access to health care facilities in nearby towns, particular groups in society who will suffer most if the clinic is closed.

Extended level candidates

Lead the discussion on to a more detailed examination of the pros and cons of each scenario. Candidates could be asked about how extra money could be raised. They could be invited to consider other important facilities often funded through government spending (e.g. nursery schools, education for older children, highway maintenance, parks and gardens, libraries) and to consider the priority each area should be given.

F Choose a Topic (Extended level candidates only)

Choose one of the topics below and talk about it for about five minutes. The Examiner will ask you a few questions when you have finished. You may take a minute or two to write some brief notes before you begin.

1 Modern technology will give us all a better and brighter future.
2 The perfect home
3 We are all responsible for our own health.
4 The place I would most like to visit.
5 There is no point in giving money to charity because it only encourages people to be dependent on others.

Development

Discuss with the candidate(s) their choice of topic and encourage them to explain and justify their ideas with reasons and examples. You may develop the discussion by offering your own comments and views. The discussion may range widely provided it remains relevant to the topic.

A Dream Holiday: Candidate's Notes

Imagine that you have won a competition and are able to choose a dream holiday anywhere in the world (bringing friends or family if you wish). What kind of holiday would you choose and why? Discuss your ideas with your partner or the Examiner. You may wish to consider:

- whether you would choose a holiday overseas or in your own country
- the type of surroundings you would most enjoy
- the sort of activities you would most enjoy on holiday
- the souvenirs you would like to bring home.

Development

Discuss with the candidate(s) the reasons for their choice of holiday, asking for specific reasons and examples. They could discuss adapting to a different climate, language and customs, if the holiday involves going abroad. Could a 'dream holiday' have hidden drawbacks such as a long and unpleasant journey, getting ill on holiday, finding people unfriendly, etc?

Extended level candidates

Lead the discussion on to the candidates' experience of entering competitions and whether they feel they are worthwhile. You could also discuss what they would ideally like for first prize if they won a competition, and why.

B Recycling Rubbish: Candidate's Notes

Your town council is concerned about rubbish in the streets and on open ground. There is a proposal to build a recycling centre for old bottles, tins and paper. Do you think this would be a good idea? Discuss your views with your partner or the Examiner. You could consider such things as:

- why rubbish can cause problems, especially in towns
- ways to collect people's rubbish for recycling
- where the recycling plant could be situated
- why some people may object to the idea.

Development

Discuss with candidate(s) the points raised. In particular, candidates should be encouraged to provide some details and reasons for their opinions. Encourage them to talk about their own town and what rubbish collection/recycling programmes, if any, are in use. You could ask them what they do at home to recycle waste, such as reusing bottles and composting. It would be useful to explore the pros and cons of building the recycling plant itself, including issues such as noise and pollution from the plant, the expense of building it, and the employment it would create.

Extended level candidates

Lead the discussion on to consider the wider issues of environmental protection, e.g. the need to reduce the number of trees which are felled for the paper/packaging industries, using unleaded petrol, protecting the ozone layer.

C The Future: Good or Bad?: Candidate's Notes

Discuss with your partner or the Examiner whether you think life in the future will be better than it is now, or worse. You may wish to consider such ideas as:

- the possibility of finding cures for diseases
- the state of the environment in the future
- how computer technology may affect people
- employment in the future.

Development

Discuss with the candidate(s) the issues. In particular, ask them for reasons to justify an optimistic or pessimistic view of life in the future. Ask for specific examples of things which could be done now in order to improve life or avert disasters in the future. You could ask candidates how much they are influenced by views of the future shown in futuristic films and in science fiction.

Extended level candidates

You could lead the discussion on to ask what could be done to ensure a peaceful future for the planet and greater international cooperation.

D Smoking: Candidate's Notes

Your town council is proposing to ban smoking in all public places. Discuss with your partner or the Examiner whether you think this would be a good or a bad idea. You may wish to consider ideas such as:

- why many people like smoking
- smoking and health
- advertising and smoking
- why young people start smoking.

Development

Discuss with the candidate(s) the points put forward, encouraging them to provide reasons and specific examples. You could ask about attitudes to smoking in their own family/community and whether banning smoking in public places would be feasible in the community they belong to. Candidates may like to consider why people may object to the proposal, and how people could be encouraged to support it.

Extended level candidates

You could develop the discussion to consider how far peer group pressure encourages young people to smoke, and the effectiveness of advertising campaigns designed to make people aware of the dangers of smoking.

E Water: A Precious Resource: Candidate's Notes

In many parts of the world it is not easy to get clean water, whilst in other places water is taken for granted and often wasted. Is a clean, safe water supply across the world an impossible dream? Discuss your ideas with your partner or the Examiner. You could consider such things as:

- the many uses of water in everyday life
- why it is important not to waste water
- what can be done to make sure people in various parts of the world can get clean water
- the importance of educating people about water and health.

Development

Discuss with the candidate(s) the issues involved, encouraging them to give specific reasons and examples. You could lead the discussion on to consider, for example, local projects which have been set up to maintain a good water supply in the community. You could also ask what could be done to help people use water more wisely, and what effect water shortages in the future might have nationally or internationally.

Extended level candidates

Lead the candidate(s) on to discuss the role governments can play in ensuring a good water supply. Your discussion could include innovations such as desalination plants. You could also discuss the need to protect water sources from contamination and pollution by industries, etc, and how this might be achieved.

F Choose a Topic (Extended level candidates only)

Choose one of the topics below and talk about it for five minutes. The Examiner will ask you a few questions when you have finished. You may take a minute or two to write some brief notes before you begin.

1 The dream that everyone will have enough to eat can come true!
2 Why I want to be rich.
3 Space research is worthwhile.
4 People who fail at school have only themselves to blame.
5 There is no point in bringing children into the world today.

Development

Discuss with the candidate(s) their choice of topic and encourage them to explain and justify their ideas with reasons and examples. You may develop the discussion by offering your own comments and opinions. The discussion may range widely within the topic, provided it remains relevant.

A Clothes: Candidate's Notes

Discuss with your partner or the Examiner your views about clothes. You may wish to consider such things as:

- the sort of clothes you normally wear
- the sort of clothes you would like to wear
- shopping for clothes
- the cost of clothes
- different kinds of clothes for different occasions
- uniforms at school or work
- the idea of 'designer clothing'.

Development

Discuss with the candidate(s) the points put forward. Where they have difficulty imagining a situation, you could supply concrete examples – for example, ask what clothes they would choose for a wedding, and why. If you discuss shopping for clothes, you could include the pros and cons of shopping for clothes by catalogue or over the internet (if appropriate). You could ask how important they think appearance is and whether it is right to judge people by the way they look.

Extended level candidates

Extend the discussion to consider the role of traditional dress in many cultures. Why has that particular style of clothing evolved (climate, cultural values, availability of local materials, etc)? Do candidates think the adoption of Western-style clothing in preference to traditional dress is a good or a bad idea? You could extend this to discuss whether being given a lot of freedom in choosing how to dress is pleasurable or creates stressful choices. You could also ask whether clothes confer power on the individual, and why.

B Food and Eating: Candidate's Notes

Discuss with your partner or the Examiner your views about food and eating. You may wish to consider:

- the kind of food you normally eat
- your favourite food
- special meals for important occasions
- convenience food
- choosing a healthy diet
- cooking food.

Development

Discuss with the candidate(s) the points raised, encouraging them to provide reasons for their views. You could develop the topic by asking them to discuss whether family meals are still an important part of family life, or whether people are increasingly choosing separate eating or 'TV dinners', and to what extent this affects our way of life. You could also discuss national dishes, shopping for food, and candidates' experiences of eating at friends' houses or in restaurants/fast food cafés.

Extended level candidates

Lead the discussion on to a more detailed examination of food in society, and the extent to which our choices about 'good' or 'bad' foods are determined by advertising and commercial interests. You could discuss whether fashionable ideas of body shape create stress for teenagers and cause problems with normal eating.

C Money and Society: Candidate's Notes

Discuss with your partner or the Examiner your views about money. You may like to consider:

- the importance of money
- pocket money or allowances
- doing a part-time job to earn extra money
- the idea of a 'fair' or 'minimum wage' for work
- saving money
- becoming rich.

Development

Discuss with the candidate(s) the points raised, encouraging them to provide reasons for their views. You could develop the topic by asking candidates to talk about issues such as: how money affects society, the advantages money brings, the disadvantages of not having enough money for your needs, ways to use money wisely, why money does not guarantee happiness.

Extended level candidates

Lead the discussion on to the role of the media in creating needs which can only be satisfied through earning more and more money.

D Children's Behaviour: Candidate's Notes

Some people say that children today do not behave as well as they should. Discuss with your partner or the Examiner your view of children's behaviour. You may wish to consider such things as:

- typical behaviour problems among children
- ways to encourage good behaviour
- punishments for misbehaviour
- how schools can encourage positive behaviour.

Development

Discuss with the candidate(s) the ideas suggested. Questions could focus on home and family issues such as arguments with siblings and parents, and how these can be resolved. Encourage candidates to relate their views to their own experiences of discipline issues.

Extended level candidates

Lead the discussion on to considering whether modern technology (TV, computer games, etc) has an effect on children's behaviour. Candidates could be asked whether children copy violence or misbehaviour they see on TV. You could also discuss wider issues such as whether over-use of computer games, etc interferes with the acquisition of self-discipline and the ability to concentrate on difficult tasks.

E Handicrafts: Candidate's Notes

Handicrafts such as sewing, weaving, pottery and woodwork play a part in many societies. Discuss with your partner or the Examiner your views on the importance of handicrafts in society. You could consider such things as:

– whether you yourself enjoy making things with your hands
– the skills required for producing good handicrafts
– typical kinds of art and craftwork in your country
– whether people are less involved with handicrafts than they used to be.

Development
Discuss the ideas suggested, encouraging the candidate(s) to provide reasons for their views. Should more or less time be spent on arts and crafts teaching in schools? Is it worth learning crafts which may be very time-consuming? Candidates could discuss the history of a particular craft in their country (if appropriate).

Extended level candidates
Lead the discussion on to a consideration of the decline of traditional skills in many countries, and why this might be happening. Candidates could also be asked about the role of museums in society, the work of any artist they particularly admire, and any art or craftwork they would especially like to own.

F Choose a Topic (Extended candidates only)

Choose one of the topics below and talk about it for five minutes. You will be asked a few questions when you have finished. You may take a minute or two to write some brief notes before you begin.

1 Everyone should learn a sport!
2 Celebrations
3 Friendship
4 The main problem with teenagers today is …
5 Self-belief is the key to a successful life.

Development
Discuss with the candidate(s) their choice of topic and encourage them to explain and justify their ideas with reasons and examples. You may develop the discussion by offering your own comments and opinions. The discussion may range widely, provided it remains relevant to the topic.

A Enjoying Music: Candidate's Notes

Some people say music is essential to life, whilst others have little interest in it. Discuss your views about music with your partner or the Examiner. You may wish to consider such things as:

- music you personally enjoy
- the reasons people have for listening to music
- different kinds of music for different occasions
- the value of learning to play a musical instrument or singing in a choir
- whether music becomes more or less important to us as we get older.

Development

Discuss with the candidate(s) the points put forward. Questions could be asked about a musician they particularly admire, whether classical music is 'better' than pop music, traditional music of the candidates' culture, and the best ways to introduce someone to music which is completely new for them.

Extended level candidates

Lead the discussion on to a consideration of the lifestyles of pop stars or famous musicians the candidates will recognise. Would they like to be one of these people? Would it be exciting or stressful to be highly paid, be constantly under the glare of publicity, travel widely and be unable to have an ordinary family life?

B You and Your Home: Candidate's Notes

'Home' may be a town flat or a house in the countryside. It may be a small cottage or a beautiful villa. Whatever type of home people live in, it tends to play an important part in their lives. Discuss with the Examiner or your partner your views about home. You might consider such things as:

- the advantages and disadvantages of different types of homes, e.g. city flats, country cottages
- what you enjoy or dislike about hour home
- what makes a house into a 'happy home'
- the kind of home you would like to have for yourself in the future.

Development

Discuss with the candidate(s) the ideas put forward. The following points could also be considered: ways to make where you live more comfortable, why arguments start about housework, why teenagers may want to have their own room at home, and (if candidates have spent time away from home) what they noticed about home on their return and their experience of homesickness.

Extended level candidates

Lead the discussion on to the role of the media in presenting us with ideas about the 'luxury dream home' and how far this is desirable or achievable. Candidates could also talk about the idea of 'roots' and the longing for 'home' felt, even after many years, by people who have left their countries or origin and settled elsewhere.

C Friendship: Candidate's Notes

Discuss with your partner or the Examiner your views about friendship. You could consider such things as:

- how we choose our friends
- the qualities that make a good friend
- making new friends
- whether making close friends gets easier as you get older
- tests of true friendship.

Development
Discuss with the candidate(s) the points raised, encouraging them to provide reasons for their views. Lead the discussion on to why we sometimes 'fall out' with friends, and how we can resolve such disagreements. Should we always be completely honest and frank with our friends, or are there occasions when it is better not to be?

Extended level candidates
You could go on to ask what sacrifices the candidates would be prepared to make for their friends. Do they think the need for friendship and being part of a group is at the expense of learning to enjoy 'your own company' and using time on your own wisely?

D The Power of Goals: Candidate's Notes

Is having goals in life a good or bad thing? What are your own personal ambitions and goals for your studies, your career, your sporting or social life? Do you eventually hope to become rich and well-known, or will you be content with a more 'ordinary' life? How are you going to go about achieving your goals?

Discuss with your partner or Examiner your own goals and ambitions.

Development
Encourage candidates to be specific about their goals, rather than just talking in general terms about 'getting a good job' or 'doing well at school'. Ask them to discuss the practical steps they are taking towards achieving their goals (e.g. voluntary work, taking extra classes, researching a field of interest). They could also discuss the value of redefining goals as their life changes or as it becomes clear a goal is no longer appropriate or achievable.

Extended level candidates
Lead the discussion on to talking about where goals come about – e.g. family pressure, the media, role models, personal reading, a need to compensate for a perceived lack – and the difficulty of shaping goals which are truly one's own rather than other people's. Candidates could also explore whether some people's goals have more to do with the associated feelings and status than with the goal itself – for example, is the goal of becoming a professional footballer largely to do with the skills of playing football or with feelings of power, prestige and success?

E Guilt: Candidate's Notes

People who cannot feel guilt are said to be dangerous, but on the other hand some people who have done nothing wrong suffer from uncomfortable feelings of guilt. Discuss with your partner or the Examiner your views about guilt. You may like to consider the following:

- why it would be bad if people could not feel guilt
- where feelings of guilt come from
- situations that trigger guilt feelings
- whether women are more likely to feel responsible for everyone's happiness and therefore more likely to feel guilty about things than men.

Development

Help the candidate(s) to explore the concept of guilt by putting forward concrete situations for them to consider. Why, for example, may forgetting your mother's birthday produce feelings of guilt but forgetting to watch a football match on TV not cause guilt? Would they feel guilty if they were jealous rather than happy when a sibling got new clothes or did well at sport? Encourage them to talk about times they have felt guilty, and why, and times when they might have felt guilty (such as not returning an item they borrowed) and didn't. Candidates could also discuss at what age children learn to feel guilty about wrongdoing, and appropriate ways to correct misbehaviour.

Extended level candidates

Lead the discussion on to the idea of irrational guilt, such as feeling guilty for situations in which we are not to blame. Candidates could consider the role of the media in manipulating guilt feelings by showing tragic photos of famine victims etc. You could also discuss ways of channelling feelings of guilt into more productive action, such as giving to charity or voluntary work.

F Choose a Topic (Extended level candidates only)

Select a topic from the list below and put forward your own ideas on it for five minutes. The Examiner will ask you some questions about it when you have finished. You may take a minute or two to write some brief notes before you begin.

1 Pets
2 'Big business' and sport – a disastrous partnership!
3 Child film stars – exploited or just lucky?
4 Food just isn't safe to eat anymore.
5 Youth and enthusiasm are much more important in the modern world than age and experience.

Development

Discuss with the candidate(s) their choice of topic and encourage them to explain and justify their ideas with reasons and examples. You may develop the discussion by offering your own comments and views. The discussion may range widely within the topic, provided it remains relevant.